Whitetail Tracks

THE DEER'S HISTORY & IMPACT IN NORTH AMERICA

Published by

 **krause
publications**

700 E. State St. ● Iola, WI 54990-0001

Please call or write for a free catalog of publications. The toll-free number to place
an order or to request a free catalog is (800) 258-0929, or use our regular
business number (715) 445-2214.
Library of Congress Catalog Number: 2001090663
ISBN: 0-87349-280-3
Printed in Canada

To my students
— *Valerius Geist*

Foreword 7

Preface 9

CHAPTER 1

A Spectacular Survivor 10

CHAPTER 2

Why Dinosaurs Count 22

CHAPTER 3

Dynasties from the Ceiling and Floor 34

CHAPTER 4

Whitetails Emerge 44

CHAPTER 5

Elephant Dozers and Predator Hell 54

CHAPTER 6

Man Meets Whitetail 68

CHAPTER 7

What Makes Whitetails Tick? 80

CHAPTER 8

Trade-Off and Compromise 98

CHAPTER 9

To the Ends of the Earth 108

CHAPTER 10

The Whitetail's Art 124

CHAPTER 11

Trophy Bucks 144

CHAPTER 12

Closing the Circle 160

Epilogue 172

Additional Reading 173

About the Author 175

About the Photographer 176

Foreword

When reading anything by Professor Valerius Geist, I often pause to kick myself for mental laziness. Geist makes me realize I'm not asking "why?" enough.

This book is no exception. While reading this fascinating account, I discovered something about myself. Namely, I might know a few things about white-tailed deer, their habits and habitat, but I knew little of the processes and evolutionary influences on the animal, its habits and its behaviors.

Obviously, my whitetail education had some huge voids. One such void is that it's impossible to interpret or appreciate the animal's actions or its world without knowing more about its rich, prehistoric background. For instance, it's one thing to correctly interpret a buck's intentions when it lays back its ears, raises the hair on its neck and body, and sidles toward another buck. Obviously, this buck is announcing its aggressive intentions, and the other buck should quickly prepare to fight or flee. But why does the buck make its body appear larger, why does it avoid eye contact with its antagonist, and why does it approach its opponent in a roundabout manner?

Geist — with his rich knowledge of plant and animal life and evolution in Earth's long history — not only interprets the buck's body language but also explains how and why these behaviors came to be part of the whitetail's being. When you view the whitetail with Geist's insights, you realize how little you truly know and understand about North America's favorite species of wildlife.

Just as importantly, you develop a broader, more vivid image of the whitetail because Geist's explanations mesh smoothly and intelligently with the photography of longtime collaborator Michael Francis of Montana. Francis' striking, full-color photos capture every aspect of whitetail behavior, be it courtship, grooming, feeding, fighting or resting. Some photographers are content to supply an editor with a cache of photos, and let the pictures impress and illustrate on their own with only a loose connection to the accompanying text. But not Francis. He and Geist collaborate not only on photo selections, but also on the captions that accompany them. They do everything possible to ensure their readers benefit from their respective contributions to the book.

With all the many impressive books available on whitetails, one might think there's no need for yet another. *Whitetail Tracks*, however, makes one realize most whitetail books are too similar and share the most damning of links: They contain little original thought or insight into the creature itself. Most do a good job of documenting and illustrating the whitetail and its world, but few explain the rich genetics, adaptations and history beneath the whitetail's grace, strength and flexible nature.

Whether you're a hunter or nature-watcher (maybe I repeat myself), it's impossible to read *Whitetail Tracks* without feeling renewed appreciation for this remarkable animal, which has been thriving in North America since eons before the first humans appeared on the continent. And even though whitetails got along fine without us, never before have they shared their habitat with a species that so obviously benefits and threatens them simultaneously.

Through Geist and Francis, you'll see the whitetail in ways you never knew existed. While doing so, you'll deepen your respect for a creature that is only slightly less adaptable in behavior and habitat preference than are we. You'll also better understand why whitetails and humans have become so inextricably linked in North America, be it in forests, woodlots, suburbia or our imagination.

No previous book has conceived or tried to explain so much about the whitetail, but Geist and Francis accomplish the task with artistic and scientific ease. You'll wonder how you watched and admired this animal so intently, yet overlooked so much.

Of course, maybe that's why Geist and Francis produced the book, and we're just reading it.

— *Patrick Durkin*
Editor, Deer & Deer Hunting *magazine*
July 2001

Preface

How is it possible that a small deer, scarce and quite insignificant in the faunas of North America for millions of years, survives all disasters and then outnumbers all large mammals, becomes a major food item almost continent-wide for natives in North America and subsequently for its European colonizers, and in modern times threatens to become the universal image for "deer"? Something terrible and dramatic must have taken place for this flip-flop to have occurred — something that turned the natural world upside down.

Yet wonders never cease! The pretty little deer explodes into supreme abundance when embraced by North America's European conquerors, it feeds their reckless conquest and nearly perishes in the process, only to rise like a fire-bird from its ashes, to not merely be resurrected, but spurred to extreme abundance. It became an idol, even to folks of opposite outlooks. It is glorified in *Bambi* by starry-eyed romantics, in spectacularly antlered trophies by starry-eyed hunters, and jealously guarded by landowners. However, it also became an object of scorn and derision to powerful scientific and urban elitists, a focus of bitter politics.

How did it happen? And why?

Read on!

— *Valerius Geist*

CHAPTER 1

A Spectacular Survivor

The yellow light of the winter sunset played on the buck's stout body and flashed in his antlers as the big whitetail dashed across a snow-covered Saskatchewan stubblefield. I had him in my sights, but did not shoot. I was not sure I could hit this fast-moving target precisely, and so I merely watched as he raced past me. With a flash of his tail, he jumped the fence and vanished into an aspen bluff. I was left standing with a pounding heart.

What a sight! I have been out many days hunting whitetails since that distant evening, the last day of deer season in 1955 and the first season I hunted. I have never again seen — let alone shot — a buck that would rival that one. I cherish the memory, the initial shock and wonder of seeing that large, graceful buck emerge from a yellow aspen grove uphill, pause and then race past me at full speed. Today, he would have been an easier target, but I was then a novice, unsure of my shooting skills on moving game. As a cadet in the Regina Rifle Regiment, I had acquired good military marksmanship on standing targets, but for hunting, that is not good enough. I turned to head back to meet my companion. The weak winter sun on the horizon was heralding the day's end. The big buck had provided a great ending to a remarkable day!

A little earlier that day, I had slowly stepped into a grove of small aspen trees. Easy does it! I advanced a step at a time, scanning ahead. The snow was reasonably soft, but still a bit noisy, and thus a slow approach was warranted. I had entered the woods with the low winter sun at my back, blinding any deer that might look my way. I was then a high school student, and, though new to deer hunting, I was a seasoned observer of deer. In fact, I had been an observer long before coming to Canada from Germany as a boy. Many fresh deer tracks pocked in the snow about me. I had high hopes. I paused to look around — and there, as if by magic, stood a 2½-year-old buck looking back at me over his shoulder, squinting into the sun. He was about 10 paces away. I slowly raised the rifle, placed the crosshairs behind his shoulder and squeezed — and squeezed — but no shot broke. I lowered the rifle to see what was wrong and, in exhaling, fogged my glasses. I could see nothing! By the time I had cleaned my glasses and

Above: South American deer have been observed making observation jumps while running. However, it appears that North American whitetails might also perform such jumps. This high-flying buck isn't crossing an obstacle. Note his highly erected head. He has a high vantage point for viewing.

discovered I had failed to release the safety, the buck had vanished. I stalked on, slowly, ever so slowly. Less than 30 minutes later, and less than 100 yards from where I had met the young buck, my eyes met those of a doe who was standing, ducked, ready to bolt, behind a willow — about five paces away! The moment our eyes met she lit out, and so did a second doe I had not seen. I stalked on. Upon leaving the aspen bluff, I glanced uphill across a snow-covered stubblefield just as the majestic buck appeared and raced past me, his tail flash closing the season.

An old trapper, Tom Walker, had taken a shine to me and, together with his son Roy Walker, had taken me deer and moose hunting that year. It was a gift of great generosity for which I am eternally grateful. I did not shoot anything that year. In fact, our first meeting with white-tailed deer was, for me, deeply humiliating. My friends shot while I, standing beside them, saw nothing! I did, however, see my first bull moose in the wild, as well as a nice white-tailed buck, but left both unscathed. The next year, however, I shot my first moose and two deer, including a fine 10-pointer that the old trapper had pushed my way.

That was the last day I hunted with Tom Walker, and I never saw him again. I left for the university, and that fine buck was the last one I took for a good many years. However, whitetails stayed in my blood, no matter where the trail led. And that trail led to some spectacular wilderness adventures in the Canadian Rockies and the Yukon Territory, when, as an apprentice-scientist, I followed the tracks and sights of big game and their predators through the seasons. The fascination with whitetails followed me into professional life and into retirement. It is still with me. Very much so!

I know more about whitetails now than I did in those Saskatchewan days nearly a half-century ago. I have studied their social behavior and ecology in the field. I have hunted them and learned much in the process. I have studied their skulls and antlers, and I have measured and compared. Above all, I can place them in perspective with other deer, or ruminants, and I can appreciate their great significance to natives and nonnatives in North America. The whitetail is quite a deer!

The whitetail is, in the first instance, a deer of great antiquity. We find fossil remains of white-tailed deer, or something awfully similar, in Florida deposits going back almost 4 million years. No other deer species can match that. That's twice as long as the Pleistocene era, fancy words for the past 2 million years of major ice ages. This ancestral whitetail appears at the beginning of significant cooling in the Northern Hemisphere, a time of considerable climactic instability characterized by minor continental glaciations. The whitetail was then a bit more primitive in teeth, which is not a big deal. It is part of an ancient fauna of many deer species whose fragmentary fossilized bones inspire unending wonder and questioning. It appears that as global cooling moved southward, the temperate hardwood forests were not unlike those on our Eastern seaboard today. However, in earlier epochs, long before the ice ages, these forests were growing in what is today the high Arctic.

When the whitetail appears in ancient pre-Ice Age Florida, the climate was building toward the big cold-warm oscillations of the major glaciations. The North and South poles were developing large glaciers and Arctic tundra was spreading south and toward lower elevations. Whitetails were apparently residents of these Northern hardwood forests, and merely followed them as they shifted south when the climate cooled.

As with other primitive species alive today, so the white-tailed deer is a spectacular survivor. Overcoming all adversities is the hallmark of biological success. Changing into a new species in response to adversity is a distant second-best. Speciation always stands for terrible times barely

I GLANCED UPHILL ACROSS A SNOW-COVERED STUBBLE-FIELD JUST AS THE MAJESTIC BUCK APPEARED AND RACED PAST ME, HIS TAIL FLASH CLOSING THE SEASON.

survived. A gold medal goes to those that survive without changing in form or function. Those are the real winners, and the white-tailed deer must be counted among them. It lived on and on as the world changed around it.

Still, whitetails show regional differences, but because expression of characteristics depends on genome and environment, it is a moot point guessing which difference is hereditary and which is not. Subspecies based on differences in body size and shape are dubious. Yet whitetails do show great genetic differences regionally, but such differences — as one would expect — do not follow current subspecific designation. As a result, I shall drop this fruitless subject from further consideration!

Note that primitiveness discussed here stands for superior ability, not for inferiority. The white-tailed deer is so successful a "form" that sub-Arctic or tropic, coastal marsh or desert, it retains the same form. We have no difficulty recognizing whitetails as whitetails wherever they are, and even experts struggle telling where a white-tailed deer is from just by looking at it. South American and North American whitetails are exceedingly sim-

ilar, even though genetically they are further apart than are North American whitetails from black-tailed deer.

There must be something awesome about the white-tailed deer's shape to have survived such genetic transformation! Put a whitetail from Venezuela beside one from Florida, and I would let you guess which is which. They are so much alike. This stability of external characteristics over huge geographic and ecological distances, despite great genetic differences, suggests if we could see a white-tailed deer of 4 million years ago we could identify it as a whitetail at once.

Four million years ago, the fauna was far different from what it was subsequently, or for that matter, what it is today. The typical North American ice age fauna of giant herbivores and carnivores had yet to assemble and evolve. South America was still an island that had not touched North America and had an ancient fauna of its own. The fauna surrounding early whitetails in North America was rich, nevertheless, but in species long extinct. Can you visualize horned camels; large raccoons; three-toed horses; American hunting-hyenas; bone-eating dogs; long-legged peccaries; mastodons with shovels for tusks; and several species of small saber-toothed tigers, primitive cheetahs and short-faced bears?

How did whitetails survive when most species about them perished? Spreading into favorable habitat and landscapes at every opportunity is certainly one way to beat extinction. That's what saved horses and camels. They immigrated to Asia and Africa while going extinct in their native North America. And whitetails knew how to spread! When South America

Below left: In Texas, white-tailed deer occupy diverse landscapes, but they do best in the most productive ones that offer seasonally abundant food of high quality. Whitetail food habits vary enormously over the huge range they occupy.

Below: Whitetails in Wyoming exploit the cover of river valleys and the fertile, irrigated fields of table lands, often forming sizeable herds. This landscape can be haunted by sudden blizzards. On the other hand, it might be hit regularly by warm winds — the western chinooks — that blow and melt away snow, exposing ground food.

touched North America, they were right there, one of the first species to step onto the land bridge and colonize South America. Consider that pronghorns, beavers, elephants, buffalo, mountain sheep, mountain goats and black bears never accomplished that feat!

How did whitetails cross the Southern deserts that appear to have kept out so many North American species from South America? And whitetails did not just venture once into South America. They did so at least twice!

The first invasion of whitetails apparently speciated with breathtaking speed and spun off new forms, dwarfs and giants. Most new species from that most ancient radiation are already extinct, such as the huge-antlered Argentinian pampas deer that vaguely resembled reindeer. Also, whitetails went the other way and quickly generated dwarf species, the brocket deer and tiny pudu. As unlike as these little South American fellows are to our whitetails, they are stunningly similar genetically.

A later invasion made modern-like white-tailed deer colonize South America all the way across the equator to southern Brazil and Peru. Because whitetails in North America reach the Arctic Circle, they span from North to South America an astonishing 79 degrees latitude. It's like having zebras extending from northern Norway to Africa.

What makes whitetails such survivors? A glance at the last huge extinction episode in North America shows that although other species vanished, white-tailed deer exploded in numbers and rushed in to fill empty spaces. Previously, when our ice age fauna was still intact, white-tailed deer remains were rare. Is it possible that what spells trouble for most species is a boon to whitetails? Are ecological disasters their very life-blood?

Early whitetails were species of warm-temperate climates, which is one reason they adapted so splendidly to equatorial conditions in South America. And yet they survived in the North when climates turned cold. As North America became home to foreign species from Asia and South America as land bridges formed — and its fauna diversified and specialized in the subsequent ice ages — whitetails carved out their niche. A predator-prey race developed then in North America, jacking up body sizes in predators and prey, and causing great specialization in both. Whitetails played right along. The main reason this beautiful deer can thrive unseen in suburbs, or can be so hard to stalk if you meet him in the habitat of his choosing, is his long legacy of escaping hordes of hungry, highly specialized predators. No Old World deer can pull off the routine antics of white-tailed deer in evading hunters. That's why stalking whitetails is the king of the hunt. It's hunting the hard way.

Regarding today's whitetails, we know a lot about them. This species is a well-researched deer. It is, therefore, easy to amass facts about this deer and still understand so little about it. For example, look at its eyes, ears and nose. All critters have such. Nothing much newsworthy here. Or is there? Compared to its close Western relative, the mule deer, the eyes, ears and nose of the white-

Below: White-tailed and mule deer fawns have some obvious differences. However, the whitetail wins the beauty contest. Its smaller features have been adopted as the universal deer image.

Right: Within a few days, the fawns — under maternal supervision — are allowed a little time to explore the world, to look about and make a first acquaintance with open spaces.

tailed deer are significantly smaller! How come? Why can the whitetail get by with less eyes, nose and ears than mule deer? Long-distance detection of enemies is apparently not part of the whitetail's survival strategy, as it is of the mule deer's. Any Western deer hunter will tell you as much.

Moreover, observe whitetails and mule deer, and the latter is much more showy, smelly and noisy. There is more to see, smell and hear about mule deer, and mule deer let you know! Compared to the shy whitetail, the mule deer overwhelms you with its sensory presence. Why? Why does the whitetail need smaller eyes, ears and nose?

Decipher that and you are on the way to "understanding" whitetails. You will then have made sense of meaningless facts. This book is not about conventional whitetail wisdom, but detective work about whitetails.

So what about noses? There is "fate" in the size and shape of one's nose. (Moose don't win beauty contests, do they?) In deer, the nose becomes disproportionately larger as body and head size increases. Small white-tails, fawns in particular, have the shortest noses; does have larger ones and the larger-bodied bucks have relatively larger noses still. That characteristic has a fancy scientific name called *allometric growth*. Small-bodied whitetails, such as island or desert forms, will have more fawn-like faces than large-bodied deer from Northern forests. We find the short-nosed versions most appealing, and label such faces "pretty," probably because they fit our innate "baby-face" preferences.

Because white-tailed bucks start out with a relatively smaller nose than mule deer bucks, even large-bodied, mossy-horned white-tailed bucks retain a "pretty face." Big mule deer bucks, by comparison, grow a large "Roman" nose. They are less "pretty," no matter how imposing!

Consequently, the white-tailed deer wins the beauty contest. Although a little smaller than those of the mule deer, the whitetail's eyes are still large enough to generate an appealing baby face. Thus, it is no an accident that Walt Disney chose the image of a whitetail for his Bambi movie, and not the Western mule deer, despite the mule deer's larger eyes, and despite the absence of whitetails from California and Disney's Western affiliation. The whitetail's Bambi image is a consequence of its smaller nose!

And what sociological repercussions that Bambi nose has had, especially when accentuated by skilled artists for mass consumption. Moreover, while we celebrate Santa Claus and his reindeer — Rudolf, especially — notice that in artists' renderings, Santa's sleigh is often not at all drawn by reindeer, but by white-tailed deer! Reindeer or caribou do not have pretty little noses, but wide, large noggins. Moreover, reindeer are often Roman-nosed as well. So guess who replaces them?

Therefore, whitetails form the universal deer image in North America. In Europe, the universal deer image is formed by the red deer, a cousin of our elk. However, that might change. In reading European weeklies, I notice with increasing frequency white-tailed deer images in advertisements. So, it appears American know-how and business practices are making the whitetail the international image of deer.

We love whitetails! In fact, whitetails are the rage today. A glance at sporting magazines will you tell you that. Pictures of big-antlered bucks fill the periodical shelves of drugstores, competing — successfully — with lurid pictures of ladies in various stages of undress. We are not the only ones who have a crush on whitetails! Apparently, native people loved white-tailed deer even more! Whitetails were the meat source in much of North America in pre-Colombian times. They are found in many archaeological sites, while other big, huntable species are rare. Natives often labeled white-tailed deer "meat," and meat was important and prestigious in their diet. They used all of a deer's carcass, even the knuckles and toe bones, which were crushed and boiled for soup, indicating just how precious whitetails were. Deer were cherished!

And yet, man and whitetails have barely met. They crossed paths when humans colonized the Americas, and — odd as it might appear — man and whitetails could have met first in middle or even South America, rather than in North

America. More on that later. Before then, humans and whitetails did not have a common history for nearly 60 million years. That's the duration of the Tertiary Period, also called the Age of Mammals, to contrast it with the preceding 150 million years or so, which was the Age of the Ruling Reptiles, the dinosaurs. Odd as it might seem, but the story of all modern mammals — the whitetail and ourselves included — begins with dinosaurs. If you want to understand whitetails, in particular their body language, which intuitively makes so little sense to us, or their body structure, or some fundamental facts about their ecology, then there is no choice but to look at the age of dinosaurs — no matter how odd it might appear. The whitetail's body language has more in common with that of coyotes and grizzly bears than with our own. That can be costly to us if we're exposed, for instance, to captive whitetails, as misunderstandings are legions! For instance, a buck might not only threaten you, but also put you at a disadvantage, and you will not know it!

Whitetails are structured to communicate differently from us, and there is an ancient reason for that. So, let's go back to that unspeakably distant time when dinosaurs were the rulers of all the land and seas. It's a must not only if you want to understand the body language of whitetails or that of our own species. This will also help us understand why today's landscapes in North America are so unusual, and why they were terribly weird ecologically, even as Columbus landed.

THE WHITETAIL'S BODY LANGUAGE HAS MORE IN COMMON WITH THAT OF COYOTES AND GRIZZLY BEARS THAN WITH OUR OWN.

CHAPTER 2

Why Dinosaurs Count

Whether dinosaurs went out with a bang or a whimper is still debated by experts. Go they did, and with stunning finality.

Dinosaurs. The very name triggers awe-inspiring images of power, mystery, fear — but also of gargantuan controversy. Yet these reptilian bird-giants were important in our appearance on Earth, as well as the white-tail's. Had not extinction swept them away with stunning finality, neither humans nor whitetails would be here today, nor the whole radiation of the advanced placental mammals. With dinosaurs usurping the dominant life forms on land and sea, mammals had no hope other than to fill the niches of small, shy insectivores and frugivores, that is, little eaters of insects, fruits and flowers. Dinosaurs were hopelessly superior to mammals, and they kept landscapes in a vegetation structure that helped them perpetuate their ruthless ecological dominance. Had not something quite mysterious killed them off, they would likely still be the Earth's dominant herbivores and carnivores, as they had been the preceding 150 million years or more.

The passing of the dinosaur and its ecological consequences are also important to understanding modern landscapes and the notion of wilderness. We are currently in another age of extinction, and we might contemplate what that means to the future. Here, the past is instructive.

Dinosaurs were terminated, some experts argue, by a giant asteroid that hit Earth some 63 million years ago. It must have been an unspeakable cataclysm. A reverberating wave of destruction of unimaginable proportions struck Earth. Tidal shock waves — tsunamis — rose from the oceans to unheard of heights and power. Towering walls of water swept away whole landscapes deep within continents, churning, ripping, plowing, flattening, grinding, drowning and trashing all in their paths. Giant trees were shredded into match sticks, searing fire storms swept the land, whole deltas were excavated and lifted far inland, mountains were ripped open, their churning rock and mudslides shredding all life. Scorching winds blew along with the floods, dispersing debris, ensuring that whatever might have stood and survived inland was blown away or burned. Dust and ashes, mixed with

Above: Western rivers carry abundant silt that was liberated in the Rocky Mountains by cirque glaciers and snow fields. The highly fertile silt is deposited as alluvium along the water courses. Abundant forage for whitetails grows in this rich soil.

Opposite: Deep snow provides some insulation and, thus, some protection for resting deer.

gravel, rocks and boulders crashed to earth from high above to bury the land, choking to death whatever the shock tides and fire storms had left standing. The storm created a long black night, save for unceasing mighty lightning flashes, while the roaring water, wind, thunder and rock falls shook the land. It was hell on Earth, and it ended the Cretaceous Period, and with it, the last of the dinosaurs, the great dynasty of bird-reptiles — warm-blooded, active, powerful — that had lasted hundreds of millions of years. Earth had been transformed from thriving life into something akin to a moon-landscape, albeit a hot, steamy and dark one, as untold cubic miles of powdered earth engulfed the globe in a black, churning cloud.

One would think that nothing could have survived this holocaust, and little did. But life went on! Bacteria survived splendidly. Plants survived not only in protected pockets deep inland or under protective shallow soil cover, but also because most of their seeds did not perish. Many aquatic animals survived far inland in deep lakes where the water blanket gave some protection. So did small terrestrial animals that hid below ground or within surviving vegetation. Large animals, be they terrestrial or marine, did not make it, but small denizens did. A "nuclear winter" chilled the land, but, eventually, the sun broke through. This hesitant sunlight was enough to spur bacteria, trigger seed germination, and inspire emerging insects and surviving small mammals, birds and aquatic organisms.

A big asteroid's impact would have terminated dinosaurs and many other forms of life. However, there are credible indications that these mighty reptiles — or were they bird-monsters? — were diminishing anyway. Some experts argue that the dinosaur's dynasty, for whatever reasons, had run its course. They were still present when the asteroid (or asteroids,

because there might have been several) struck. They still filled the niches of giant herbivores and carnivores. They were probably still quite abundant, but their species diversity had shrunk. The dinosaur lineages that previously had been actively speciating were no longer filling new ecological professions or niches. They were failing to adapt and were dying out. Not surprisingly, families that evolve frequently are troubled families. They have a poor capacity to adjust and are, therefore, struck frequently by severe natural selection, which often leads to a new species, which is merely a temporary success before oblivion. Species that do not evolve are the real evolutionary success stories, and whitetails are an ancient species indeed. However, when the dinosaurs vanished, whitetails — and humans, for that matter — were still far into the future: some 60 million years, give or take a few millions.

So, how are dinosaurs relevant?

CANOPY OPENINGS LET SUNSHINE IN, AND A SPOT OF REJUVENATING FOREST FLOOR ECOSYSTEM IS FORMED.

The bang that finished dinosaurs started us. That cataclysm, unspeakably large on the human scale, had — on the ecological scale — merely rearranged the nutrients! It rejuvenated the land ecologically. It freed nutrients from previously living bodies and thus fertilized the land. It set back ecological successions to basic levels. The scarred landscape was set for a quick and lush flowering, and life exploded again into the familiar struggles to do one better on the competition. However, there was a big difference now, compared to the intact, undamaged world before the asteroid impact. In this new world, there were no megaherbivores. The huge, tree-crunching giants were gone, a profound departure from normal landscape ecology! That's crucial! Kill the big plant-eaters and continents sprout forests! It's like banishing scissors from your head and allowing your hair to grow unchecked. There had not been such forests previously, not with gigantic dinosaur herbivores around! That was the new setting, the new ecological stage, for a new beginning for life on Earth.

Old-growth forests shade out earth. Big herbivores let sun shine in, warm the earth, and let the soil burst forth a diversity of life. Continuous old-growth forests are, on a geologic scale, short-lived because giant herbivores re-evolve and return global ecosystems back to normal. Trees struggling to evade huge teeth and herbivores striving to eat up trees represent Earth's normal state of affairs. The dinosaur megaherbivores were especially noteworthy! The horned triceratops, duck-billed dinosaurs, and the last of the brontosaurs were not only huge but probably the most efficient megaherbivores to ever walk the Earth. For grinding vegetation, they had large, ever-growing tooth-plates or bird-like gizzards lined with grinding stones. They had enormous, powerful bodies to push over and break trees or break or bite off branches, and huge body cavities that indicate gigantic fermentation vats to break down plant cellulose into fatty acids and sugars. Some, like

the duckbills, might even have ruminated like cattle or deer. We might never know, but we can be certain the huge guts and caeca of big herbivorous dinosaurs were almost constantly rumbling from methane gases, and that they passed a lot of gas and huge, steaming heaps of dung.

The only trees to survive the carnage megaherbivores inflicted were those that could rapidly resprout from broken trunks or roots, or could vigorously regrow missing branches and stems. They could also spread rapidly to areas with a bit more light to grow faster and larger. Vegetation had been conditioned to quickly repair itself and spread quickly because of hundreds of millions of years of severe browsing and breaking by huge plant-eating dinosaurs. After the dinosaurs disappeared, there must also have been a great extinction of tree species. Not only did the seeds of some tree species depend on passage through the guts of megaherbivores for sprouting, but fierce competition for space and light soon choked out species that owed their existence to regular, predictable opening-up of the landscapes by huge herbivores. The sun, by heating the soil, stimulated rapid degradation by bacteria and fungi of all organic matter. And such degradation liberates the nutrients locked up in dead wood and, above all, in the mass of dead leafs on the ground.

Take away the tree-crunching dinosaurs, and an age of trees begins. Dense, dark, tall, majestic forests smothered the land, snuffing out all but the smallest openings, blocking the sun's rays to the soil. In the absence of megaherbivores, forest fires burning in dense, continuous forests must have been large and severe. Fires replaced giant herbivores as devourers of trees. Where megaherbivores ruled, they kept down forests, opened up the landscape, removed much of the vegetation before it could turn into dry

Above: After the rut, bucks exhausted by fighting, breeding and roaming, hide and rest to regain their strength. They must heal infected wounds, which is one reason they frequently look haggard and listless.

Above: Plants sprout vigorously where land and water meet, creating what is known technically as riparian plant communities, such as this cattail swamp in western Montana. Whitetails closely follow riparian vegetation.

tinder as fuel for fires ignited by lightning storms. With megaherbivores, wildfires were small, infrequent and benign.

Most trees are repeatedly browsed and broken, repeatedly set back in their growth until, with a sudden growth spurt, they escape one summer to shoot upward. Ultimately they tower as invincible giants that send wave upon wave of seeds far into the land. The breaking and browsing by giant herbivores ensured tall, massive, well-rooted trees that could resist being pushed over by giant bodies. It also ensured well-spaced trees and closely cropped meadows and shrubs. This is not favorable for fires to ignite or to burn with large, hot flames, which can turn the very soil into ash.

Megaherbivores were followed by a long ecological coattail. They generated biodiversity. Their continuous browsing, leaf-stripping, breaking and uprooting of trees and shrubs; their deposition of huge piles of dung; and their trampling and scratching of soil stimulated plant productivity. By these means, these herbivores conditioned the landscape so a high diversi-

THE TYPE OF
LANDSCAPES WE
TAKE FOR GRANTED
AS "NATURAL" ARE
ACTUALLY AN
ARTICLE OF HUMAN
INTERVENTION
CAUSED BY HUMAN
ELIMINATION OF
MEGAHERBIVORES.

ty of plants and animals could thrive. Inadvertently, they created food chains that rose from massive dung deposits, or depended on dinosaurs digging for subsurface water in sun-baked riverbeds.

The megaherbivores co-evolved with plants that depended on the hot bellies and roaming legs of these tree-shredding monsters to disperse their seeds. The seeds of many trees, shrubs and herbs must pass through a herbivore's gut before they can sprout. Entire families of tree-species die out when their seeds no longer pass through the stomachs and intestines of big herbivores. Many insects and birds also depend on the body surfaces of megaherbivores for their food, be it to feed on blood, scabs, skin debris and secretions, or insects and parasites on the skin.

Whatever gravity ordains, megaherbivores opposed it, as they churned up the land, crisscrossed it with deeply worn trails that acted like trenches for draining downpours. This prevented shallow flooding and, thus survival of land-hugging small mammals, birds and invertebrates. Soils trampled by hoofs formed myriad tiny puddles after a shower, within which invertebrates reproduced, and were avidly consumed by swarms of birds. The dead bodies of megaherbivores fed diverse megacarnivores, scavengers and insects, which, in turn, fed birds, small mammals, insects and other invertebrates. Megaherbivores turned the monotony of dark, dense, old-growth forests into sun-lit, ever-renewing, species-rich diverse ecosystems.

Above: The buck tears the bark with its antlers, which tend to collect bark fibers. Not only does the buck deposit scent from the skin glands on his forehead, but he also licks the horned site, and might nibble the frayed bark.

Above Opposite: In fall, Northern fawns stop growing and fatten for the harsh winter ahead. They have to rely on themselves from now on.

After the big asteroid bang, megaherbivores did not return for some 10 million years. By then, the great, tall forests had given rise to many new life-lines, including some that run to you and me and the whitetail.

Life adores opportunity. It simply will not rest! Survivors of the great extinction at the end of the Cretaceous period quickly went about making the best of the situation. Dense, closed forests are rich in evolutionary opportunities. They provide a huge biomass of edible, digestible matter. However, the spatial distribution of this biomass is complex and daunting. As trees strive for sunlight they — of course — grow tall. They spread their crowns way up there. And up there they grow tender shoots, flowers and fruit. Birds, bats and insects have it made. They can readily exploit such towering riches. In a sense, a rich, productive photosynthetic layer is supported high above the ground on tall pillars. For terrestrial beasties, this means the layer is available to those that can really climb and stay aloft "glued" to branches and twigs. However, to get to the flowers, fruit and shoots — which more than likely grew on thin branches — requires a small body. Consequently, empty niches for small fruit and shoot eaters are begging to be filled. Ditto for small-insect eaters, because productive canopy layers abound with such. Given continuous old-growth forests stretching across continents, evolution will hurriedly generate a lot

of tree-top acrobats.

Of course, fruits and seeds are not much good to a tree unless they reach the ground, where they might sprout, set roots and grow into another tree. That is, seed fall and seed sprouting are mandatory parts of forest ecosystems. You can make, therefore, a good living staying on the ground and feeding on what trees shed — which is much more, of course, than seeds and fruit. Every wind storm breaks branches, which fall to the forest floor, as do lichens, mosses, insect pupae, eggs and nestlings, and dying birds, reptiles and mammals. Not everything is highly digestible, though, such as a tree's thick bark, woody branches and certain old leaves. These, however, are consumed by microbes and insects. Thus, the forest floor concentrates bits of highly digestible food, be it through fall from the canopy or through sprouting or providing ecological opportunities to earth-bound scavengers and saprophytes. However, although such foods can be reliable, they are not abundant. Productivity — the annual growth of leaves and seeds of the old forests — is ultimately low, despite enormous amounts of nutrients stored in the trees' trunks, roots and canopies. Trees gravitate toward storage, not production, of new branches and leaves, as do trees cropped by megaherbivores. Only when a giant tree slams to the forest floor is its canopy available as food to the small folks on the ground. Canopy openings let in sunshine, forming a spot of rejuvenating forest ecosystem. That means more quickly digestible food, and thus more opportunities for the little forest floor scroungers.

And that is what evolved in the wake of megaherbivores: forest-floor scroungers. However, because forest-floor edibles are limited, so is the number, size and density of forest-floor scroungers. Moreover, because food is limited and precious, it is worth defending. Therefore, forest-floor scroungers are notoriously "territorial," that is, they defend a piece of real estate for their exclusive use. They can be nasty creatures. They might tolerate a mate, but even their children they tolerate minimally. Parents kick them out as soon as possible, so the adults can reproduce again. Offspring that are kicked out must try their luck elsewhere or die. And many do die!

Forest-floor scroungers thus defend the resources they need for life within a defended space. We call this space a territory.

Tree-top acrobats and forest-floor scroungers concern us because our roots lead back to the former and the whitetail's to the latter. The deep, extensive, connected space of the forest canopies allowed little tree shrews to evolve into a great dynasty, the order *Primata*, our order. Extensive forest floors allowed a plethora of small scroungers to evolve, among them what was to become the great dynasty of the cloven-hoofed herbivores, the order *Artiodactyla*. Whitetails are *artiodactyls*, as are sheep, goats, cows, hippos and pigs. Human roots are deeply imbedded in Old World primates. We owe our origins to the ecological accident of continents densely covered by trees — which didn't have dinosaurian megaherbivores demolishing them. Although this situation arose from an accident of nature, it was a happy accident. Thus, we arose from a temporary, terribly screwed-up ecosystem. Maybe the dinosaur extinction was a good thing, for without their going, the natural processes that led to current times and our existence could not have unfolded. Death is not only a prelude to life, but also to novelty. We are certainly a novel form of life, a form so novel that we can contemplate dinosaurs. We might dream of those fascinating bird-reptiles, but such a dream is only possible because they died, because their extinction literally "caused" us to arise via a rare ecological aberration — continuous continental forests.

From that ecological aberration, not only we arose, but also many other mammals, reptiles and birds. However, the post-

Opposite: Productivity is often associated with water, and whitetails follow productivity. Here is a white-tailed buck in a cypress swamp in northern Florida.

Below: Exuberant antler growth can be the result of superior feeding and artificial selection for antler growth. Although such bucks might have antlers of breathtaking proportions, they are a handicap when escaping from predators.

dinosaur era, the Tertiary Period, is an "Age of Mammals," because mammals — not birds or insects no matter how rich in species — formed the megafauna again. Birds tried hard, for sure. Quite a few gigantic bird species — terrestrial and marine — followed the Cretaceous, the last age of dinosaurs. However, mammals won out this time, both on the land and in the oceans. The new crop of tree-eaters was not quite as efficient as those it replaced, nor were the mammals capable of evolving giant carnivores to match those of the dinosaur past. They did a bit better in the oceans, populating these with fish-like whales, a life form few dinosaurs ever assumed. Tropics dominated till the ice ages came around and produced a crop of unusual creatures, of which humans are good examples. What dinosaurs gave with their passing was, thus, the gift of life. Death is always a beginning.

And that takes us back to body language. Forest-floor scroungers retained the old body language, but tree-top acrobats evolved a new one. Whitetails, like all mammals that arose from forest-floor scroungers, retained the ancient body language in which an individual communicates with the broad side of its body and averts its eyes. Primates do not. By virtue of addressing one another while sitting on the same branch, primates shifted their center of communication to their face and ventral body parts. That's what another primate on the same branch can see. In other words, primates look at each other! We do not avert eyes, but make them central to all face-to-face communication. We no longer have any intuition about what it's like to communicate with the body broadside and eyes averted. It means nothing to us, yet it means everything to four-legged land mammals! It's a difference that leads to gross misunderstanding even by modern biologists, a misunderstanding that has led to death and injury for people dealing with whitetails.

As to landscapes? Have you noticed anything about our landscapes, or about the presence of megaherbivores? Tall, continuous forests dominate our current landscapes. That's a consequence of removing megaherbivores. And guess who removed megaherbivores worldwide for the past 10,000 years? You guessed it! We did! We also, of course, currently disrupt forests via clear-cutting, be it for wood products or to make space for homes and agriculture. The landscapes we assume are "natural" are actually an artifact of human intervention, because of human destruction of megafauna. To live in unadulterated "natural" landscapes would be to live with a fantastic array of huge herbivores and carnivores. Therefore, none of today's landscapes are natural. In fact, they're highly unusual landscapes — even without clear-cutting, agriculture, highways and urban sprawl.

THE TERTIARY PERIOD IS AN "AGE OF MAMMALS" BECAUSE MAMMALS, AND NOT BIRDS OR INSECTS, FORMED THE MEGAFAUNA AGAIN.

CHAPTER 3

Dynasties from the Ceiling and Floor

The bang that finished dinosaurs started us. We came from a terribly screwed-up, temporary ecosystem, namely from flourishing, continuous forests that covered continents from shore to shore. Kill the big-plant eaters, and continents will sprout forests. It's like banishing scissors from your head and allowing your hair to grow unchecked. So it was with continents without giant herbivores. Continuous old-growth forests shaded the ground. Big herbivores let the sun shine in, which let the soil burst forth with a diversity of life.

Continuous old-growth forests are, on a geologic scale, short-lived, because giant herbivores re-evolve and return global ecosystems to normal. Trees struggling to evade huge teeth and herbivores striving to eat up trees are the normal state of affairs. However, it takes a few million years to get there. It took about 10 million post-dinosaur years for giant plant-eaters to again crunch trees, but this time they were mammalian, not reptilian giants. Moreover this new crop of tree-eaters was not quite as efficient as what it replaced. Nor were these mammals capable of evolving giant carnivores to match those of the dinosaur past. They did a bit better, though, in the oceans, populating these with fish-like whales, a life form few dinosaurs ever assumed.

Nevertheless, the Age of Mammals, the Tertiary period — which followed the last dinosaur age, the Cretaceous — was probably less extreme in biological diversity. That is until the ice ages came around and produced a crop of unusual creatures, of which you and I are good examples.

Thus tree canopies gave rise, among others, to primates both in the Old World and the New World. And we descended from primates in the Old World. The forest floors gave rise to various dynasties, foremost among these were the cloven-hoofed Artiodactyla. We, as primates arising within lofty canopies, were always a bit closer to heaven than deer and their ancestors. And, as it turned out, we needed to be! Whitetails arose from artiodactyl forest-floor scroungers, but not before some of these scroungers gave us haughty, lofty, stuck-up primates a scary run for our

money. It came about as follows.

Artiodactyls are universally characterized by a unique heel articulation. When we find a fossil with such an articulation, we know we're dealing with an artiodactyl, no matter what the rest of the body looks like. The earliest artiodactyl were not merely ground-hugging forest-floor scavengers, they were developing the art of the fast get-away. They had to. Other forest-floor scavengers had shifted their food habits and began scavenging scavengers, along with other delectables they found. They were becoming carnivores. We call these early carnivores the *creodonts*, and there were lots of them. They did very well in the millions of years that followed dinosaur extinction. That means scroungers that favored plants, such as the whitetail's ancestors, were constantly running and jumping for their lives. Especially jumping. That's when their unique heel construction came into its own, helping them become airborne between big hops. Very long hops!

A few escapees, however, did more than run away in high bounds and then hide somewhere, befuddling the carnivores. A few made a point of jumping up to branches, hanging on, and climbing to a safe spot in the tree. Early on in the game, ground-dwelling artiodactyls were able to do that because they had good "hands" and muscular arms. Their legs were starting to become specialized for running, especially their hind legs, but the front legs remained versatile all-around tools with fingers that could grasp. In fact, the front legs stayed that way for some time and changed into specialized running legs only slowly, as if reluctant to do so.

Therefore, some early artiodactyls did exactly what primates did: They found climbing in trees to be a safe, rewarding experience. Along with security, there was food up there, plenty of leaves, shoots and fruit. So, these early tree-hugging artiodactyls specialized for climbing. They evolved long-tailed, cat-like bodies and climbing legs. Moreover, these "tree-deer" were eminently successful for millions of years. They stood up to us primates! But ultimately, they could not compete against ecologically aggressive primates. The arboreal artiodactyls died out, while our primate dynasty, tree-bound for almost all its long history, prevailed.

Predation pressure on the forest floors was relentless. It selected for ever-better means of escaping predators and for quicker reproduction while holding on to good pieces of habitat to successfully raise offspring. Eventually, that generated a small- to medium-sized ground dweller that had large, muscular haunches. These big muscles powered the long jumps.

SCROUNGERS, SUCH AS THE ANCESTORS OF WHITE-TAILED DEER, WERE CONSTANTLY RUNNING AND JUMPING FOR THEIR LIVES.

The back also became heavily muscled, because it enhanced body flexure and added power to the haunches. The legs became sturdy and elongated, especially the hind legs, for ever longer, higher bounds and faster speed. Now the legs ended in small, hard hoofs, which are most conducive for running and dodging on hard, lateritic tropical forest floors.

This bounding-running mode is called *saltatorial running*. Because food in good habitats was dense enough to be defensible, the artiodactyl saltatorial food scroungers armed themselves with long, sharp canine teeth. These were used primarily by the male to defend his food territory against others of its species. Only his chosen female was safe from attacks. We thus see early in the Age of Mammals a slow progression toward small, saltatorial, well-armed herbivores. We call this particular type of adaptive strategy the duiker of slinker syndrome.

Duikers are actually small African forest antelopes. Their name graces the forest-scroungers' adaptive strategy. It was, or is, found not only in antelopes, but also in deer, pigs, rodents, other bovids, and in many more

early forms, including early horses and their relatives. The duiker body form was the starting point for a series of new radiations, artiodactyl and others. However, the artiodactyls turned out to be a virile order. Not only did it branch into bovids, deer, giraffes, pronghorns, tragulids, camels, peccaries, pigs, hippos and a bag full of extinct lineages, but also into whales. While one branch of pigs went for dry land to exploit underground food sources, and a second branch, the hippos, went into fresh water, a closely related third line went to the seashore, and from there into the ocean. They evolved into whales.

Are whales marine-adapted hippo-pigs? Yes, they are, just as the pig is the whale's equivalent on land! Pork bacon and whale blubber have the

RIVERS ARE THUS OASES OF LIFE AND, FROM A DEER'S PERSPECTIVE, THEY DO SO MANY GREAT THINGS! THEY PRO-VIDE BIG PULSES OF SUPERLATIVE FOOD.

same genetic root. Genetically, the order *Cetacea* (whales) vanishes because whales are but a branch of the artiodactyls, branching out — to be precise — between pigs and hippos. Thus, DNA research can tell a lot about the wonders of descent. However, it can tell us nothing about adaptation, and adaptation matters when tracking whitetails — or humans.

After all, who would think whales or porpoises are brothers of pigs or cousins of whitetails? The reason why this is so bizarre, so incomprehensible, is that whales and porpoises have adapted very differently from pigs or white-tailed deer. Adaptations make us unique, not the individual genes we carry. For these we share with an infinite assemblage of living things, including bacteria, protozoa, plants, insects, fish and fowl — you name it.

Above: When running in tall grass, white-tailed deer progress by a saltatorial running mode, that is, they run in tall bounds. This is an expensive way to move, and the deer must seek cover for hiding. The whitetail's Pleistocene home was the fertile southern coastal plains, which were covered in tall grasses.

We are only dimly aware of what happened on the long road the whitetail's ancestors took so long ago. The past holds firmly to its secrets. After all, after the asteroid bang, it took about 60 million years before recognizable white-tailed deer appeared on Earth. It took another 2 million for something one could label "human" to stand up, and another 4 million years for modern humans to people the earth. However, in a crude sort of way, it appears that deer — having evolved into small-bodied duikers — hung on for a long time. They refined their adaptations as scroungers on tropical forest floors, but added nothing that was startlingly new.

However, that in itself was significant, for primitive deer refined how to exploit damage to ecosystems. Rivers, for instance, tear a rift through the forest, ripping out trees, swilling away the soil, demolishing with each flood the shore vegetation, and depositing mud and debris along the flood plane, especially in oxbows. Rivers are terribly destructive, especially big rivers, rivers prone to flooding, or rivers that freeze and gouge out beds and shorelines with ice blocks. Read, sometime, what Mark Twain wrote about

the mighty Mississippi. As a riverboat pilot, he saw the river's carnage first-hand. Read what he wrote about its floods, new channels and the perpetual movement of huge sand beds. Twain wrote all about it in fascinating detail. Rivers bundle incredible destructive powers, and the bigger the river, the greater the power.

However, ecological destruction is always the beginning of something new. Floods clear the land of competitors and store water in the flood plain. The mud is very fertile. Water, fertility and open spaces favor plants that come in quickly, and then rapidly and massively sprout, spread, flower and fruit. These plants grow so vigorously that bare ground is soon lush with greenery, more so than unflooded land. These aggressive or pioneering plants produce seeds copiously, so that all but a few plants can be demolished without hurting their species' survival. Rivers are thus oases of life and, from a deer's perspective, they do so many great things! They provide big pulses of superlative food. Exploit these pulses and you can grow a lot of big, vigorous babies. The deeper the river digs its bed, the better. The banks have varying aspects, that is, exposures, to the sun. And that means plants sprout first on southern slopes, next on eastern and western slopes, and finally on northern slopes. Moreover, vegetation communities vary with location and compass direction. As a result, deer can exploit a richer variety of food by visiting different areas of the banks and fertile flood plains. Where flood waters are not severe, some trees survive. These trees, generously watered and fertilized, produce fine food for deer in their foliage, especially if the seasonal foliage dries and sheds annually. Bacteria and fungi pounce on shed leaves, fermenting them into ensilage — a superb, long-lasting deer food. And if a creature can dash and jump, the riverbed's steep banks are great protection from predators. The animal can run to the steep slopes and jump up into thickets or cliffs, a most effective way to escape.

Best of all, carnage done by flooding rivers only prepares deer for a much greater carnage: big forest fires. And without megaherbivores to disperse and shred trees and bushes, thus cleaning up potential fuel for fires, the vast post-dinosaur forests must have been haunted by gargantuan fires. These could quickly turn the burned land into a moonlike landscape, except that, ecologically, destruction is always a beginning. Forest fires set into motion easily predictable recovery processes. These are so predictable and distinct that ecologists speak of ecological successions that follow burns. Ashes do the same as silt in the rivers: They fertilize the ground. Flames do the same as the flood: They clean out all competing vegetation, clearing the ground for a new flush of vegetation. And that early vegetation is low to the ground and, thus, quite available to small herbivores. Also, it is very nutritious and plentiful. Moreover, it stays plentiful, nutritious and available for years. The early plant succession stages following forest fires are heaven for herbivores.

Because rivers flood regularly, we designate ecosystems perpetually rejuvenated by flood and mud as *pulse-stabilized* ecosystems. Forest fires caused by lightning can be expected but not predicted. One cannot state when and where they will burn, nor how large the fire will grow. However, they happen often enough that it pays for some herbivores to adapt to

exploit them. Such herbivores produce large numbers of young. These must be capable dispersers so as to capitalize on the early years of abundant low-growing, nutritious plants. Eventually, of course, burns revert to normal old-growth forests. However, that takes many decades. Climax forests are poorer habitat for deer, and deer must adjust by living conservatively within their means — till the next forest fire hits.

The valleys of flooding rivers, of course, remain excellent habitat because they are ecologically rejuvenated almost annually. Thus, deer that evolved to exploit pulse-stabilized flood-plain ecosystems are

also able to quickly take advantage of similar ecosystems, whether these ecosystems are caused by floods, fires, storms, avalanches — well, you name it! The big generators of ecological successions are, of course, floods and fires, and we can be reasonably certain that fires were common and large once old-growth forests sprouted all over the world after the dinosaurs' demise.

Deer, it so happens, stuck to opportunistic exploitation of ecological disasters, rather than specializing in severe inter- and intra-specific competition for food. This made deer rare in mature, species-rich ecosystems, but common after competitors died out in major extinctions. For this reason, we find deer fossils relatively rarely, and for that reason, the course of their evolution during the long Tertiary period is poorly known. When the ice ages came along with their cataclysmic climate and great ecological changes, deer, as lovers of ecological havoc, spread and multiplied. They did even better when another destructive force emerged on Earth — man.

However, that event lay still millions of years into the future.

Above: As specialized pack-hunters, gray wolves can overcome many of the anti-predator defenses of native North American deer and have eliminated deer regionally. Wolves currently enjoy endangered species status and are expanding in many regions where white-tailed deer are found.

Opposite: Coyotes, although effective predators on fawns, normally have a difficult time downing adult whitetails. Coyotes are one-third the size of a large gray wolf, and do not routinely hunt in packs. Here, a coyote pulls down a buck ill with epizootic hemorrhagic disease.

CHAPTER 4

Whitetails Emerge

As a result of tall continental forests that followed the extinction of dinosaurs, early mammals split into forest floor scroungers and acrobats. The floor-adapted lineages went through a fantastic diversification, evolving ultimately into huge herbivores and carnivores. However, there were always tough little forest floor scroungers, and one of them gave rise to deer about halfway through the Age of Mammals about 30 million years ago.

Those early deer were a successful lot that spread across the Northern hemisphere. Antler growth predisposed them to food rich in protein, calcium and phosphate, which was abundant in fertile habitats. Fertility is concentrated in disturbed landscapes, seasonal landscapes and ecologically immature landscapes. Therefore, deer loved living along flooding rivers, deltas and seashores. They loved frost and the great boost it gave their food supply. Consequently, whitetails prospered and multiplied as the Earth's climate cooled, heralding the ice ages.

White-tailed deer emerge in North America's fossil record about 4 million years ago, appearing suddenly in the southern portion of the continent along with other deer. You might say they arrived "out of the blue." However, a closer look makes it appear less miraculous. Virtually the entire northern portion of North America was ground by nearly two dozen continental glaciations over the past 2 million years. Mile-high ice polished millions upon millions of year's worth of rocks, obliterating every geological record down to the age of the dinosaurs. There is no way to know from the fossil record what happened in most of northern North America in the past 65 million years or more because the fossil record was eaten away by the ice.

However, the very northern portions of the continent were much less glaciated or not glaciated at all. Portions of Alaska, the Yukon Territory and some high Arctic islands escaped continental glacia-

There, we find good samples of fossil records that are missing in glaciated areas. The high Arctic islands are particularly interesting. There, large tracts of flora were fossilized, showing clearly what happened to plants during the Tertiary and Pleistocene periods. These floral deposits are superbly preserved. Unfortunately, no matching animal or faunistic deposits exist. The reason for this resides in the nature of fossilization. Floral deposits were preserved under acid conditions, which greatly favored the preservation of cellulose. The same conditions dissolve bones. However, these plant fossils remain tantalizing. They show that warm forests existed where today we find an Arctic desert, and those forests changed to temperate forests 4 to 6 million years ago, resembling today's forests on the North American East Coast. In short, 4 to 6 million years ago, the high Arctic was superb white-tailed deer habitat. Sad to say, the bones of forest dwellers were not preserved. We know that beavers were present because beaver dams and tooth marks

Opposite: The Eastern hardwood forests are an ancient homeland of white-tailed deer. Such forests can be traced back for millions of years and to higher latitudes when climates were much warmer than they are today.

Below: In eastern North America, moose and white-tailed deer have an uneasy coexistence — if they coexist at all! White-tailed deer have coevolved with the brain worm, giant liver fluke and winter tick, all of which highly damage moose, caribou, elk and even mule deer.

MUCH LATER TO
APPEAR THAN
WHITE-TAILED DEER
ARE MOOSE, CLEARLY
A COLD-ADAPTED
LINEAGE THAT
NEVER WENT INTO
WARM CLIMATES.

CURRENTLY, WHITE-TAILS EXPLOIT THE URBAN SAVANNAH WE CREATED AND THE AGRICULTURAL LANDS THAT SUSTAIN US. THEY JUST ADJUST, FIT IN AND THRIVE.

were preserved. Someday, fossilized deer tracks might be discovered, or even a bit of deer bone. Till then, however, we are left wondering what inhabited the temperate woods of northern North America during the late Tertiary period.

We noted that in the late Tertiary period, climatic deterioration led to the huge cold-warm oscillations of the ice ages, which are known as major glaciations. The late Tertiary saw the beginning of minor glaciations about 4 to 5 million years ago. Thus, as minor glaciations escalated toward major glaciations, the Northern temperate forests moved south. As they moved far to the south — beyond what was to become glaciated terrain — these forests and their inhabitants appeared in the southern half of the continent about 3 to 4 million years ago. That is when deer, white-tailed deer included, appeared for the first time. In short, deer must have been present in Northern temperate forests all along. If so, we expect most warm-adapted deer species to appear earlier in the late Tertiary fossil record, and the cold-adapted deer species to appear last. And that's exactly what we find.

White-tailed deer appeared first. They adapted to climates warm enough to allow them to spread across the narrow Central American isthmus into South America. Here they and related deer species gave rise to an explosive deer radiation. These movements generated — among others — rock hoppers in the Andean mountains (huemal, taruka), palmate-antlered giants on the Argentinian pampas that distantly resembled caribou, dwarfed forest floor scroungers throughout the continent (brocket deer and pudu, the smallest of all deer), gregarious herders on the savannah (pampas deer), big swamp deer with long, spreading hoofs and other species whose fossils keep us guessing what they were. Whitetails spread in northern South America as a species well beyond the equator and diverged genetically from North American white-tailed deer more than North American white-tailed deer did from our black-tailed deer.

Much later to appear were moose, clearly a cold-adapted lineage that never went into warm climates. Despite their grotesque size, moose are actually surprisingly close relatives of white-tailed deer. Next to appear — but in

the Old World — were roe deer, which have many adaptations indicative of a long evolution in cold, long winters. Last to appear were reindeer, which showed up first in Alaska and only at the beginning of the major glaciations — a sure sign we are dealing with a master of cold adaptations. In short, we discover fauna that evolved in temperate forests at high latitudes in late Tertiary North America and Siberia when these forests shift south with increasing cold and aridity on the Northern pole. We are entitled to suspect that these vast Northern forests were the home of deer during much of the warm Tertiary Period, while to the south, many warm-climate floras and faunas evolved. These began to shrink in size and diversity as the cold pulses pushed their habitat into increas-

Above: Where secure, whitetails gravitate to fertilized areas such as lawns and fields, irrespective of equipment and machines.

Opposite: Well-fertilized cornfields are a whitetail's dream habitat, and tall corn provides excellent cover to boot.

ingly smaller areas in southern North America, leading eventually to the great extinctions of the late Tertiary. Deer, on the other hand, spread, and a couple of million years later even went into South America as soon as a land connection was formed with North America.

The first deer we find in southern North America are clearly of *Odocoileus* origins, and the late Bjoern Kurten, a famous pale-

ontologist, identified them as white-tailed deer. We can state only
that these remains, which are about 3.9 million years old, are probably ancestors of today's white-tailed deer. They are similar to
white-tailed deer, but as we shall see, white-tailed deer experienced
selection pressures so profound that it almost certainly reorga-
nized thoroughly, no matter the similarities to these ancestral
whitetails. These are currently labeled *Odocoileus brachyodontus*,
because their teeth are lower crowned than today's whitetails. This

suggests that the earliest *Odocoileus* depended more on browse and soft foliage than do today's whitetails. Grasses played a smaller role in diet than they do today. These old whitetails would have depended more on hiding, and probably were poorer at running than their descendants. They must have been shy dwellers of thickets that seldom ventured into meadows.

If age indicates success, then whitetails are extremely successful. They existed before our ancestors had barely begun their descent from the trees to the fertile ground of the African savannah. The whitetail hit upon a winning combination of adaptations that saw it through the roughest periods of the ice ages, and so it prospered even when we had shaped the land to suit our taste and vision. Although other species perished, whitetails took advantage of us. Currently they exploit the urban savannah we created and the agricultural lands that sustain us. The whitetail just adjusts, fits in and thrives. It is dawning on some of us that, like humans, whitetails are not habitat-specific but are great "adjusters" that do well wherever there is food and a place to hide. Humans and whitetails are a species "without an ecological niche." The whitetail's current strength is its ability to thrive along with man on man-made landscapes.

Another indicator of success is the whitetail's enormous geographic distribution throughout North and South America. However, what is most significant about this distribution is its utter defiance of extreme climates! The white-tailed deer ranges literally from the sub-Arctic in Canada's Yukon and Northwest territories, to 18 degrees south of the equator in South America. Snow, ice, blizzards, blistering heat, humidity, swamps, alligators, boreal forest and wolves — never mind! The white-tailed deer has adapted to them all. There are tropical whitetails that never get out of their red summer coat, and high-mountain whitetails in the Andes that skip the summer coat all together. There are island dwarfs and dispersal giants differing five-fold or more in body size. And yet in external appearance, they differ little! We have no difficulty whatsoever identifying them as white-tailed deer. And I suspect that we would have recognized the earliest whitetail in the fossil record as a white-tailed deer, were we able to lay eyes on him.

Opposite: Whitetails, at home below Wyoming's Devil's Tower, as well as in the nearby South Dakota Black Hills, use a diversity of forbs and shrubs, and the shelter of canyons and coulees. This is a dry land where mule deer are found among well-spaced, towering ponderosa pines. However, the diverse shelter, feeding opportunities and permanent small-water courses support often-dense whitetail populations.

Below: Whitetails choose obstructions to hide behind, be they natural or man made.

CHAPTER 5

Elephant Dozers and Predator Hell

It's strange to think of America as a land of elephants, even though the fossil record abounds with these curve-tusked giants and elephant dung balls have been found beautifully preserved in a dry cave in Arizona. It is equally wondrous that we can go into the forest for a picnic or hike, that we can let children play in the open or sleep carefree in flimsy tents, and that we take it for granted we will see the light of day each morning. We live in an unreal world. Our lives have never been so secure, judging from what life was like in the distant past — particularly in North America.

The world of the whitetail then was vastly different from today, surrounded as it was by many huge herbivores and carnivores, the latter quite keen on getting something to eat. Had you gone for a hike in late-glacial North America some 20,000 years ago, you would not have gotten far! The "freedom of the woods" that we enjoy today and take so utterly for granted is a consequence of exterminating most of North America's late-Pleistocene fauna and keeping the remaining small predators low in numbers and deeply frightened of our presence. It's a benefit whitetails also enjoy and exploit. However, whitetails also depended on the megafauna and its continuous ecological rejuvenation. Here, American elephants played a crucial role.

American elephants were tall and exceptionally long-legged. They are called Columbian mammoths to differentiate them from the closely related but smaller and cold-adapted woolly mammoth that roamed from Alaska and northern Canada and from Siberia to England and France. Colombian mammoths actually symbolize a time when whitetails did not have it as good as they do today. That time was the Pleistocene, the ice ages, a time of major glaciations. At that time, whitetails lived mostly in mature, species-rich, but predator-limited faunas surrounded by truly grotesque beasts. Consequently, they were not abundant during the ice ages. Their population exploded only after the extinction of American megafauna. In short, when the competition and the super predators that mercilessly pursued whitetails for 2 million years were gone, whitetails spread out geographically and multiplied in burgeoning numbers. So did black-tailed deer and peccaries, pronghorns and black bear — all very old Americans.

When examined closely, it is evident that white-tailed deer ecology is based on ecological havoc, on the destruction of mature ecosystems. Such destruction is followed by vibrant, productive ecological successions. Early ecological successions produce abundant high-quality food. This food thrives where the sun hits moist, fertile ground, where life-giving rays make forbs and bushes sprout luxuriantly. Here, the whitetail's food is rich in proteins, fats and minerals, but above all, it is diverse and available year-round. Here white-tailed does bear big, bouncy fawns, and can synthesize rich, creamy milk in abundance. Here, whitetails flourish. It all depends on the sun hitting moist, fertile soil! That's a most important, if not chief ingredient, of whitetail habitat.

Rich, moist soils are soon overgrown by vigorous shrubs, trees and occasionally tall grasses. When that happens, the sun can no longer warm the soil. It's no longer the best habitat for deer. Flooding rivers, fires, avalanches and wind storms were always present and could be counted on to destroy old vegetation and rejuvenate ecological successions by generating good food and shelter for whitetails. North America's violent climate also played its part. No east-west mountain range blocks cold Arctic air

Right: The leaves of many shrubs and trees — as well as some herbs — provide good amounts of protein and minerals to support antler growth. The high nutrient requirement of antlers has kept deer from colonizing grasslands.

Below: Twin fawns are common. By the time they are out together, fawns are already well developed and able to flee and hide from predators.

IT ALL DEPENDS ON
THE SUN HITTING
MOIST, FERTILE
SOIL. THAT'S A
MOST IMPORTANT,
IF NOT THE CHIEF,
INGREDIENT OF
WHITE-TAILED DEER
HABITAT.

from flowing swiftly south across the continent and freezing vegetation in passing. Nothing halts warm southern air masses should they venture north and unload their moisture in crushing torrents. Nothing stops air masses from mixing and sending tornadoes along tornado alley. That's true during interglacials. However, during glaciations, Arctic air might have been held behind towering glaciers. Fossils provide evidence that a surprisingly warm climate prevailed south of the ice.

Moreover, the land must have been continually fertilized by wind-borne rock dust, or loess, as is its German name. Glaciers grind up rocks and spew them out with water. Much is carried away as silt in water that slowly fills huge proglacial lakes along a glacier's margins. However, much rock dust is exposed to the sun. It then dries, and is easily picked up by even a light breeze and carried across the continent. Where it drops, it fertilizes. Thus glaciers continually rejuvenate soils with their rock dust, massively counteracting the leeching of nutrients that robs fertility from unglaciated lands. Soil richness is why whitetails thrive there, but can't on the leeched out soils of Africa. Neither could other deer. Glaciers have utterly spoiled us with fertility, and where glacial rock dust accumulated, we find today's great bread baskets of humanity.

Although important, climate is not the only habitat-creating factor. Not at all. Throughout its long history, the whitetail probably depended heavily on huge herbivores for food and shelter. The bulldozers of the Pleistocene were tall, massive elephants, squat mastodons — often as large but more massive than Indian elephants — and ground sloths, some of which were the size of elephants. These were the living wreckers and cranes that pushed down trees or ripped off big branches, opening up the canopy for sunshine to reach the ground. They left torn tree branches half-browsed, allowing whitetails to feed on nutritious, toxin-free twigs, buds and foliage. Trees protect themselves from being eaten by pushing toxins into leaves and bark, but they do so less on top, which is one reason fallen tree crowns are desirable for deer. The crashing of trees being ripped apart by a herd of mammoths or a family of ground sloths probably meant dinner for whitetails. It was a sound to run toward, just as whitetails have learned in our time that the sound of chain saws means dinner, and that loggers are harmless, no matter how loud they might be. Whitetails gather around trees downed by loggers like they probably congregated around trees downed by mammoths, mastodons and ground sloths. Just as whitetails benefited from clearings opened by giant herbivores, so they benefit today from clearings created by storms, forestry, agriculture and fires.

B y crushing and ingesting masses of woody food of low digestibility, giant herbivores also left behind masses of dung. These dung piles were not left randomly. Rather, they piled up at resting and watering areas, creating unique soils and faunal communities over time. Huge dung balls from elephants, mastodons and ground sloths — as well as high dung piles from stallions of various horse species — favored the germination of specific plants. Dung was a source of sprouting seedlings for small mammals and birds, as well as a heaven for insects. Masses of fermenting dung meant local fertility, a high production of insects and snails, and a big effect on the number of insectivorous birds and their predators. When the American fauna of megaherbivores and carnivores collapsed, so did a vibrant bird fauna. One can only wonder at the large number of small hawk species retrieved from the tar pits of Rancho la Brea, an indication that many insects, small birds and mammals were devoured by these avian predators when the megafauna were around.

Elephants and mastodons not only generated food for whitetails, but also water. When summer's heat desecrated the land, when creeks and rivers dried, elephants could always be counted on to dig below the riverbed to expose water. When they left, plenty of smaller customers were also able to quench their thirst from craters dug by the giants.

The huge megaherbivores also made wide, well-trodden trails in the thick understory, creating gorgeous pathways for whitetails to escape along if predators appeared — and appear they did!

Left: White-tailed deer search out ecological hotspots with high productivity, such as plants that grow in the wake of forest fires, illustrated here by a burn in Montana's Glacier National Park. For a decade or two — before climax species invade the burn — deer find excellent food and cover that they respond to with vigorous body and antler growth, high reproduction and dispersal.

Below: Wilted leaves in fall, such as the maple leaf consumed by this young buck, might be an important food source. Chemical analysis shows fallen leaves can be surprisingly nutritious.

During the Pleistocene period, North America was a predator hell-hole without peer that severely shaped predators and prey. Following in the wake of a mammoth nursery herd was almost certainly a clan of lumbering saber-toothed tigers, waiting for an opportunity to ambush a straying juvenile mammoth. They would quickly bring it down, then kill it with a jugular-slicing bite. Speed was of the essence for these massive cats, because the mammoth herd would quickly be upon them, and woe to the sabertooth too slow to evade the powerful legs or bone-crushing blows of the coiled trunk! A superficially wounded mammoth calf would be well-protected, and would heal, leaving big cats hungry. Therefore, a quick killing throat-bite was essential. The big cats only needed to wait out the mother's grief as she guarded her dead calf. And then the cats had dinner! Young and old, crippled and healthy. A young mammoth's carcass provided more than enough food for all. For saber-tooth cats, that was crucial. Their many broken and healed bones show they attacked their prey with such ferocity and power as to break bones and cripple themselves. In addition they must have occasionally caught bone-crushing blows from their prey. That did not matter, however, as long

Below: Wolverines, the largest member of the weasel family, are hunters and scavengers. Here, one has found a whitetail washed up by a spring flood.

Right: Research on black bears in the past decade has shown they are enterprising, versatile and successful predators. However, they also clean up winter kills, as this Minnesota black bear is about to do. After black bears emerge from their winter dens, carrion is an important food source. Soon, this bear will be feeding on new vegetation and whitetail fawns.

as the cripple could have his fill and the clan had enough healthy adults to kill big prey, so there was food left over for convalescent individuals. Saber-toothed tigers had hyoid bones in their larynx similar to a lion, indicating they were quite vocal. They were probably not only loud, but also very quarrelsome as revealed by skeletal injuries that match their sabers. They were assertive beasts that would, for instance, usurp the carcasses of elephants and bison mired in tar pits — and there die themselves in large

THE PLEISTOCENE
ERA OF NORTH
AMERICA WAS A
PREDATOR HELL-HOLE
WITHOUT PEER
THAT SEVERELY
SHAPED PREDATORS
AND PREY.

numbers and in all sizes, from kitten to broken-toothed gummer. For whitetails, these loud-mouthed, ill-humored, muscle-bound killers were of little threat, as long as they were kept under surveillance. White-tailed deer can avoid charges and, in modern times, even rocket nets and arrows.

There was a great collection of predators to make each day interesting. More dangerous to whitetails than the big saber-toothed cats was the equally large scimitar cat. That one did not roam about in loud-mouthed

Above: A white-tailed deer is a small morsel for a large wolf pack. Snow is a considerable handicap to white-tailed deer, but less so to wolves, which have enlarged paws with webbed toes — adaptations to snow, water and soft tundra.

Opposite: Northern coyotes have it much easier if deer venture on glare ice, as did this button buck. Sharp deer hoofs do not grip glare ice. However, had the ice been covered by frozen snow, as is normal in winter, the footing would have been good enough to allow the little buck to escape.

clans, but was probably a silent, solitary ambush hunter. It was a totally different cat, elegant in shape, with a head poised on a long neck. Lightning fast in its attack, it used its deadly bite to kill with surgical precision. It also had enlarged upper canines, but these were not the thick, curved daggers like those of the sabertooth. These upper canines were thin, fragile, broad, plate-like and very sharp. The scimitar cat was most likely a gut-spiller. It was a fast sprinter that must have run along its prey and, with a quick, precise bite, sliced its flank wide open, allowing the gut to spill out. In seconds, the fleeing prey had its hind legs tangled in gut and the large blood vessels from the gut to the liver ripped open. The prey died quickly. It had to, because this predator was far too fragile to engage in fight or resistance and its thin canines could not strike bone. Nevertheless, it would not miss an opportunity to ambush and bring down a tasty white-tailed deer. Whitetails had to be on guard!

There were still other cats to contend with! Large, maned lions, like those from Africa only twice as massive and very fast sprinters. Although these lions probably focused on herds of long-horned bison, horses, camels and guanacos, they could hardly have been averse to taking a toothy whitetail. Moreover, this predator hunted in groups, which is very effective. To get out of a tight squeeze, whitetails had to become agile, lightning fast, and excellent spatial planners to execute an escape.

There were also big jaguars hiding in thickets. These were probably interested mainly in peccaries, be they the large flat-headed peccary, the equally large long-nosed peccary, or the small-collared peccary. Jaguars are generalists that figure out how to catch and eat what's available, and they are not overly fussy. Where they co-exist with whitetails today, jaguars are less of a threat than cougars. However, it paid to be on guard, just the same.

In the open meadows and plains, the large American cheetah was on the look-out for tasty morsels the size of a whitetail. It specialized in the fleet-of-foot from the open plains, such as pronghorns, horses and bison calves. But then, whitetails tend to be in the open every so often. The large cheetah, over time, almost certainly improved the whitetail's acceleration and running speed.

There was the ever-present puma, a specialist in ambushing deer, various pronghorn species, or anything else that might be tasty and available. Acute attention to immediate surroundings, coupled with lightning-fast responses, were crucial. The cougar honed those qualities to perfection in whitetails, making the whitetail the high-speed acrobat it is today.

Nor were ocelots, lynx and bobcats to be underestimated. Whitetails had to be prepared for all of these predators, and many more.

Late in the last glacial period — the Wisconsinian glaciation — whitetails encountered red wolves in the East and coyotes and packs of big dire wolves in the West. Post-glacially, they ran into gray, or timber, wolves that had crossed into North America from the Bering Land Bridge along with elk, moose, grizzly bears and humans. These wolves could justly be called Siberian "snow dogs," because, like "snow deer" or caribou, they have enlarged, webbed paws to traverse soft tundra, swampy terrain and soft snow. They are also terrific swimmers that can quickly overtake swimming prey and dismember it in deep water. In earlier times, within the ice ages, whitetails confronted many wolf species. Most were coyote-like in size and appearance, but a few were large, though light in build. Early on, a wolf-sized, but massive hyena-like beast called the bone-eating dog existed. In addition, whitetails dealt with the Johnston's coyote, a whole slew of wolf-coyotes, Armbruster's wolf, Cedazo dog, dholes and Troxell's dog — as well as coyotes and red, gray and dire wolves. Some were pack-hunting super-predators, like the elegant dhole or red dog, which still survives in the Old World. Yet the whitetail bested them all! Most wolf-like predators came and went, but the whitetail survived and thrived. Some of the late ice-age wolves must have been a sight to behold!

Take the dire or grim wolf. These were big-headed, squat wolves with massive jaws and teeth, that were equal in body size to gray or timber wolves. They were somewhat more heavy-set and had more robust bones. They were built for power, not speed, as are gray and red wolves. Dire wolves were probably pack hunters that could inflict terrible bites or tenaciously hang on and quickly render large prey helpless. I suspect they hunted in large packs that could overwhelm even huge long-horned

THERE WAS A GREAT COLLECTION OF PREDATORS TO MAKE EACH DAY INTERESTING.

bison. Dire wolves must also have been efficient scavengers that crushed large bones with those powerful jaws. They appear to have been brazen and single-minded when confronted with potential food, because they readily jumped to their deaths in tar pits and trap cave sites. These caves were deep holes that horses, camels, mammoths, bighorn sheep and other animals fell into.

A pack of dire wolves would almost certainly displace other predators from a kill, or clean up abandoned kill sites. They were probably as efficient in predation as pack-hunting coyotes and gray wolves are today. Maybe more so! Fossilized bones of predators from the Pleistocene of North America — dire wolves included — reveal a high frequency of healed cracks and breaks, although the teeth are severely worn or damaged. Life must have been hard for those predators, because they were often confronted by large-bodied prey that were clearly pugnacious and violent in self defense. However, predators had to succeed in subduing such prey if they were to live. The specialization of North American Pleistocene predators and of prey to escape predation is testimony to the severity of predator-prey relationships in this megafauna.

In addition to cats and canines, there were also native North American bears that could and probably did prey on white-tailed deer. Low on the totem pole of power and always in danger from larger carnivores was the black bear. It survived the megafaunal extinctions and spread widely thereafter. Black bears are immensely intelligent — even cunning — and thus inventive in exploiting foods. Circumstances permitting, they are highly competent predators. They were not to be trifled with, even though

Below: Whitetails can overcome their innate fear of man and integrate themselves into suburbia. In some yards they are welcome, and quickly discover this. In others, they are loathed as a pest, where they destroy gardens and tree plantings quickly.

Opposite: A concentration of food, such as a haystack, attracts white-tailed deer. Although scenic and pretty, this intruder will urinate and defecate on the precious hay, making it unpalatable for cattle. Because whitetails can be persistent and skillful in getting around obstacles, it takes high fences of excellent quality to keep them away from hay.

black bears normally avoid confrontations. The black bear is a night predator that would have easily taken down deer — provided it could stalk close — and then catch it with a rush.

Three species of short-faced bears lived at this time, and all were larger than the black bear. The largest was the enormous bull-dog bear of the plains, probably the most dominant predator in its fauna. Standing taller than a Kodiak bear, this monstrous bear must have been a sight to behold. Most grizzly bears standing on their hind legs would not reach the shoulder of a large bull-dog bear male. Its face was not dished in like a grizzly bear, but short-jawed and Roman-nosed like a lion. Moreover, it was tall-legged, a fast sprinter and probably a most agile one to boot. The bull-dog bear probably sprinted to its prey, grabbed on and wrestled it to the ground. Hence, its powerful jaws. The great size of the male compared to the female indicates great breeding rivalry among males. It must have had a nasty disposition. Moreover, being carnivorous, it must have been hungry most of the time, and was single-minded and brazen in the pursuit of a meal. Its skeletons, like those of dire wolves, are common in trap cave sites. Bull dog bears were attracted by the smell of decaying flesh and jumped in and died there after their last meal. Grizzly and black bears are not found in trap cave sites, which suggests they were smarter. However, a few died in the more treacherous tar pits.

Although the bull-dog bear was probably interested in prey larger than a whitetail, its smaller forest-adapted cousin of the Southeast was probably an opportunistic hunter of whitetails, especially fawns. The large Florida short-faced bear specialized as a vegetarian and showed many features similar to those of the European cave bear.

White-tailed deer had to have a superb system of safeguarding fawns, because every predator would catch them if they could, including red fox, badger, fisher, jaguarundi, and later, the wolverine and grizzly bear. These two were late-comers, although wolverines appear to have come and gone from North America several times during the Pleistocene.

Hyenas? In the early Pleistocene, North America was home to the American hunting hyena, *Chasmaporthetes ossifragus*, Hay 1921. It was a slender-limbed, cheetah-like sprinter, highly specialized as a predator of whitetail-sized prey. Never mind, white-tailed deer survived these, too!

White-tailed deer were thus surrounded on the ground by many predators. However, there were also predators in the air and water. During the Pleistocene, several very large condor-like birds of prey existed in North America. Today, it is difficult to determine if they were purely carrion feeders and if they fed on fawns and small deer. Golden eagles are aggressive hunters that have taken fawns. However, shrubs and trees can foil aer-

FORESTRY, AGRICULTURE AND URBAN SPRAWL HAVE REPLACED ELEPHANTS AND OTHER GIANT HERBIVORES AS DESTROYERS OF FORESTS.

ial predators. In Southern waters, alligators pose a threat to whitetails, and in tropical areas, whitetails must also evade large snakes such as the anaconda or boa constrictor.

Today's white-tailed deer have it much, much easier! They live in an impoverished fauna, an odd mixture of old indigenous species that survived the great extinctions at the end of the last ice age and an influx of East Siberians that found the ecological vacuum left by megafaunal extinctions irresistible. Forestry, agriculture and urban sprawl have replaced elephants and other giant herbivores as destroyers of forests. Megaherbivores all but vanished. Only the bison and moose qualify as such — but only barely. Moreover, the swarm of swift and effective predators is gone.

Could we have survived this concentration of diverse predators? It might surprise, but the answer is no! Ancestral humans could not survive North America's late-ice-age predators. White-tailed deer could! They outdid us, for they survived North America's predator hell-hole. Humans, on the other hand, could not colonize North America as long as it was occupied by its native megafauna. When humans entered North America permanently, the native fauna was collapsing and key predators were gone. Moreover, man colonized this continent slowly, keeping pace with vanishing megafauna. Evidence of human occupation in the form of fire-places increases at the same rate per thousand years as the decline of native American megafauna. Thus, human populations kept pace with the decline of large native mammals. It is a sobering testimony to the white-tail's effectiveness in escaping predators! Whitetails outdid humans!

WHITETAILS OUTDID US, FOR THEY SURVIVED NORTH AMERICA'S PREDATOR HELL-HOLE.

CHAPTER 6

Man Meets Whitetail

It took a long time after man set foot on North America before he and the whitetail met. This is not because of the great distance from the Bering Land Bridge, which linked eastern Siberia to Alaska, to where whitetails lived in southern North America. True, people — along with elk, bison, moose, grizzly bear and gray wolf — crossed that land bridge. However, that happened long after the first human set foot on North America. Humans used the Bering Land Bridge to enter the Americas only at the end of the last glaciation, about 12,000 years ago. At that time, continental glaciers were melting rapidly, modern tundra and boreal forests replaced the glacial "mammoth steppe" in Siberia and Alaska, and North America's unique fauna of giant herbivores and carnivores was on its way to extinction. However, it is likely people tried to enter North America much earlier.

This suspicion is caused by indications that humans prospered in Mexico and South America much earlier than in North America. Several credible studies suggest that humans were in Mexico and South America as early as 30,000 to 40,000 years ago. The oldest accepted human campsite is not in North America, but at Monte Verde in Chile. It closely coincides with the last glacial maximum. There are also suggestions that mammoth hunters of the Great Plains, who exterminated the Colombian mammoth, came from the south, not from Siberia and Alaska. How could people possibly have come to South America from Asia, virtually bypassing North America? That's where some controversy resides. Moreover, the earliest human skeletons in North America — dating back to glacial melt-off and megafaunal extinction — are Ainu-like people, or ancient Caucasoids.

Big waves of humanity swept across much of the Earth 40,000 to 60,000 years ago, which is when Australia and Japan were settled. That was only possible for people with a fairly advanced understanding of building and using boats, because they had to cross miles of choppy seas. Much happened during an extended period of global warming in the middle of the last ice age. It was no full-blown interglacial period, like the one we live in, but a much shorter warm period called an *interstadial*, which lasted more

Above: Texas whitetails and turkeys have been fellow travelers for millions of years.

than 5,000 years. Nevertheless, there must have been significant glacial melt off. Consequently, water poured into the oceans, and the oceans covered the continental shelves with shallow water, thus creating warm, productive seas. Moreover, glaciers had liberated — and continue to liberate — huge quantities of nutrients that were swept into the warm shallows. In short order, shallow seas and estuaries became very productive, which stimulated people in coastal areas to exploit the surplus of rich marine resources. Technology was needed, and it is very likely that people with that technology were the first to reach North America tens of thousands of years before its ultimate colonization by the ancestors of today's American Indians.

These early boat-faring people were not the ancestors of American Indians, who came quite late, crossing from Siberia to Alaska after the last ice age. Rather, these pioneers must have been ancient Caucasoid people who were the ancestors of Japan's Ainus, Australia's aboriginal people and Indo-Europeans. These ancient people probably originated in North Africa's desert during the last interglacial. They had been bottled up at the

beginning of the last ice age, some 80,000 years ago, by the invincible Neanderthal people. The latter occupied the Mediterranean shorelines with the onset of the last glaciation, and displaced a people with a distinct stone blade culture, called pre-Aurignacean. That blade culture is the signature of our modern ancestors from the Upper Paleolithic age of Europe. The early pre-Aurignacean people, however, did not stay bottled up, but were able to skirt around Neanderthal through what is now Palestine, and pour into southern Asia. That happened during the height of the first glacial advance about 60,000 years ago. It was a time of maximum glacial growth and desiccation in Africa. With the eastern shores of the Mediterranean under severe desert conditions, only a desert-adapted people could pass. Once past the eastern Mediterranean, they could spread into southern and central Asia. When global warming began about 40,000 years ago, they spread and colonized many new areas, but not yet Europe where Neanderthal held out.

Global warming did not favor Neanderthal man ecologically, and when modern people showed up in Europe about 30,000 years ago, they slowly

Right and Below: Ecological hotspots for white-tailed deer are not only found in the wild, but might also be man-made. Agriculture, forestry, urban development, city parks, golf courses and transportation corridors attract whitetails.

eliminated the once-invincible Neanderthal man within a few thousand years. That happened in western Eurasia. Earlier, in the East, with the warm interstadial generating productive shallow seas and coastlines, these early coastal explorers went eastward into China and Japan and perhaps America. They must have repeatedly tried to establish themselves in North America, and might have done so only to be displaced by late-coming Paleo Indians, as suggested by the skeletal characteristics of Kenwick man and other fossils in North America with Ainu-like characteristics. These Ainu-like people also were displaced from China and nearly all of Japan.

Unfortunately, there is a problem gathering evidence about these early people: The coastline where these pioneers lived is now covered by several hundred feet of ocean water and lies far off shore along the continental shelf. During glacial maxima, the oceans were more than 400 feet (130 meters) lower than today. After all, we live in an interglacial age when the water that was once tied up in huge glaciers on land has melted and run off to the oceans, thereby raising coastlines. Large areas of land that were home to early man during the ice ages are now hidden by the sea. Undersea archaeology might throw some light on this ancient coastline, but don't hold your breath! As ocean shores moved inland, the pounding of ocean waves ensured the virtual destruction of surface features. Old campsites were annihilated. On one hand, much evidence about human life has been destroyed by wave action and is covered by ocean water. On the other hand, areas where humans lived during interglacial times were ground over by glacial masses. The only sites we can investigate for evidence of humans are literally between glacial end moraines and the deep blue sea! Where we hunted and danced during the ice ages is mostly covered by

NORTH AMERICANS BECAME SUPERLATIVE HORTICULTURISTS, RAPIDLY DOMESTICATING AND ARTIFICIALLY CREATING NEW "UNNATURAL" PLANTS, FOREMOST AMONG THEM CORN.

water. Where we hunted and danced during the warm interglacials has largely been scrubbed out by the advance of glacial ice. To prove, therefore, that people exploiting coastal resources advanced from Asia to North America along continental coastlines is a daunting task.

We noted earlier that entering North America some 35,000 years ago would have been virtually impossible for humans. North America was not habitable for humans because of an abundance of giant, bold and hungry predators. These could not be eliminated with the weaponry of the Upper Paleolithic. Imagine what it must have been like for a boat of these pale-faced, bearded hunters to pull up to Alaska's shores, only to see a swift bull-dog bear running to meet them! This was a tall predatory bear, as tall as a moose at the shoulders. It was the king of predators during the late glacial — swift, bold, inquisitive and brazen. A bear larger than a polar bear with those attributes would have spooked any potential immigrant, and rightly so. How do you safely kill so large a predator? The late paleontologist Bjoern Kurten, whose life work was the study of the extinct cave bear, argued convincingly that humans did not kill cave bears, but only the smaller brown bear that we call the grizzly. The bull-dog bear was even larger than the cave bear! Spears armed with sharp flint or obsidian blades likely shattered on bone. From the front, the vital organs are almost completely protected by bone. Moreover, should a narrow-bladed throwing

PADDLING CLOSE TO
SHORE, THE SEA-
FARERS SAW A
DAINTY DEER FLASH
ITS TAIL AND DIVE
INTO COASTAL
SHRUB WITHOUT
GIVING THEM A
CHANCE FOR A
CLOSER LOOK.

spear penetrate the body, it would take a very long time to kill. It leaves the bear enraged and able to pursue and destroy the hunter. That's what Spanish horseman experienced with grizzly bears. Bears are hard to kill with primitive weapons and are dangerous when wounded. It can be done with a broad-bladed, hand-held boar spear, provided one has many dogs to engage and distract the bear. Can you see people, crammed into small boats, carrying packs of dogs with them just to distract a bull-dog bear? Not likely. Moreover, there is scant evidence that dogs were human companions 35,000 years ago.

Where was it safe to be on the coast? Imagine encountering a group of bull-dog bears quarreling over a beached whale, or seeing huge American lions pace on the beach, or a horde of quarrelsome saber-toothed tigers or dire wolves. Small islands just off the coast were probably the only land unvisited by scavenging large predators. These early boat people might not have been too interested in terrestrial wildlife anyway. They probably ate a lot of kelp, birds, fish, berries, sea food, sea mammals and some plant food. There is a lot to eat along a coast. The giant elephants they saw on shore or bathing in the surf, the massive mastodons browsing in estuary marshes, the huge ground sloths breaking off limbs and stripping foliage, the long-horned bison and swift horses — all these potential food items were probably mere objects of curiosity, as were the first deer they saw. These first

Right: White-tailed deer and pronghorns have had a long association. Both are original North Americans that survived the great extinction of native American mammals at the end of the last ice age. Both are also short-lived ecological opportunists with high reproductive capacities.

deer were coastal blacktails, similar to today's Alaska Sitka deer. However, early pioneers would not have seen one until reaching, roughly, the latitude of today's Washington coast.

These bearded sea-farers probably saw whitetails on the coast of what is today southern Mexico. It is likely that this first meeting of man and white-tail was quite anticlimactic. Paddling close to shore, the sea-farers saw a dainty deer flash its tail and dive into coastal shrub without giving them a chance for a closer look. Well, what else is new? It might have taken some time before they saw another whitetail, because with all the predators and competitors still in place, whitetails were scarce. The sea-farers would have seen many more bison, camels, horses, mammoths, mastodons and ground sloths than whitetails. Moreover, they would not have hunted white-tailed deer. It was much too dangerous to wander inland and make a kill, which was a sure recipe to attract lions, bull-dog bears, saber-toothed tigers and packs of dire wolves. And why bother? Living off the coast would have been much more productive and safe. White-tailed deer became a hot item tens of thousands of years later after virtually all megafauna were extinct. Then, a new people — the ancestors of American Indians — were hard up for food, and New World agriculture developed rapidly to fill hungry stomachs. Then, and only then, did white-tailed deer become truly important in the food economy of native North Americans. All this is told by the archaeological record.

Is it not ironic? A small deer, scarce and insignificant in the faunas of North America for millions of years, survives and becomes a major food item continentally. Something terrible and dramatic must have taken place for this flip-flop to occur — something that turned the natural world upside down. Let's overview some complex happenings.

The last glaciation is waning. Temperatures are rising, glaciers are melting, oceans are filling, huge proglacial lakes are draining and evaporating, productivity on land is increasing. About 13,000 years ago, a sharp climatic reversal — called the Older Dryas in Europe — begins. The remnant glaciers covering Canada are now too low to hold back masses of cold Arctic air spilling over and traveling south across North America. Every time that happens, ponds, lakes, creeks and rivers are quickly frozen and covered by ice, making water inaccessible. When this happens, there is no snow on the ground. I have seen minor events of this type in Alberta, and wildlife is then in deep trouble. Ice thirst! Desperate thirst! If the continent were blanketed like this for a few weeks, a mass die-off of large plains animals would occur, hitting large predators the hardest. As expected, megafaunal remains are now rare, and the American cheetah and bull-dog bear disappear. With the next warm pulse, megafauna recover and multiply. Elephants, horses, camels and bison are abundant.

Man enters the scene about 12,000 years ago, this time, however, as an able hunter of terrestrial mammals. In less than half a millennia, humans eliminate mammoths, then switch to mastodons and long-horned bison. With the Colombian mammoth extinct, other wildlife — bound ecologically to elephants for millions of years — rush into extinction. Fires flame across the continent, a sign of human activity. Grazers and desert forms go extinct. Woodland species, like ground sloths and mastodons, hold their own for a while. Then they go, along with holdouts such as the dire wolf and lion. Mastodons survive human entry for almost 7,000 years, but dis-

appear during our interglacial's temperature maximum (Altithermal) about 7,000 years ago. We find their last remains high in the mountains of Utah. The mastodon was the last of the giants to go. The bison was transformed — probably by human hunting — from a long-horned giant to a short-horned dwarf. But it survives! Siberian invaders such as elk, bison and grizzly spread. Fires haunt the continent. A new cold spell, Europe's Younger Dryas, repeats in part what happened in the Older Dryas. With the next warm spell, however, the native fauna decline progressively as human activity increases. Out of some 50 to 60 species of native large mammals that lived in North America, only the whitetail, blacktail, pronghorn, peccary, bighorn sheep, mountain goat, jaguar, puma, black bear, red wolf and coyote survive. A good part of America's bird fauna also vanish. Life is becoming hard for humans. The hot Altithermal desiccates the land and forces people into agriculture, a sign of starvation. North and South Americans become superlative horticulturists, rapidly domesticating and artificially creating new plants, foremost among them corn. Horticulture spreads widely in southern North America. Although hunter-gatherers show signs of food shortages like short stature and asymmetrical body build, agriculturists grow to respectable size and symmetry and increase in number. North America is peopled, and advanced cultures begin to rise — paralleling similar developments in Eurasia and Africa. Agriculture and horticulture are incompatible with large mammals. The remnants of surviving large mammals shrink into isolated distributions. Bison, elk, moose and bears become rare and sporadic in the archaeological record. With megafaunal extinction, forests cover North America — just as they did after the dinosaur extinction. Agriculturists, without access to massive machinery, skillfully use fire to clear forests. They use it to foster the kind of biota they desire — the berries, nuts and tubers they love most. Native horticulturists are so sophisticated and skilled that modern scientists and botanists in Central America collected in native gardens, believing they were in the wilderness. When our brightest and best perform such flops, one wonders what escaped the captains, priests and soldiers who were the first to lay eyes on the lives of American people?

Burning, in principle, encourages wildlife, especially white-tailed deer. In much of North America, these deer became the primary large mammal being eaten. The whitetail was greatly relished by natives. It was not domesticated, because white-tailed deer — unlike sheep, cattle, camels or even reindeer — do not lend themselves to domestication. Nor is it necessary. Plus, it is much too costly in time and energy. It is more intelligent to foster deer through habitat management and collect them as needed. Hunting is also easier than animal husbandry. Europeans domesticated species of big game that lent themselves to domestication. White-tailed

IS IT NOT IRONIC? A SMALL DEER, SCARCE AND INSIGNIFICANT FOR MILLIONS OF YEARS, SURVIVES ALL AND BECOMES A MAJOR FOOD ITEM FOR NATIVES IN NORTH AMERICA.

deer do not. And so, in pre-Colombian North America, a small, once rare and insignificant deer, became abundant and important as a major provider of meat for native people.

Time does not stand still. Who would have foretold the incredible events that befell North America after Europeans "discovered" the Americas? The continents were whiplashed ecologically. As Europeans found a foothold in North America, European diseases and genocide almost swept away native North Americans. Tribe after tribe vanished in the 16th century. A well-populated continent began to empty of people. The heavy hand of the red man disappeared, and nature quickly took over. Wilderness spread. Very soon, gardens, fields and settlements were overgrown. Forests quickly regrew. Buffalo and other big mammals, rare less than a century before, increased in number and spread. For two centuries, wilderness spread and prospered. Explorers who penetrated the continent marveled at the abundance of wildlife and thought that was how it had always been. Americans Indians also rallied. Horses came into their hands and new cultures based on the horse began to spread. America was wild, underpeopled and in the grip of nature. Wilderness spread, an artifact of European colonization.

By the late 18th century, the heavy hand of the white man descended and virtually ended it all. North America was fully colonized by Europeans, suppressing Americans Indians. Wildlife was commercially exploited to near extinction by the end of the 19th century — white-tailed deer included. This devastation brought about a continental rethinking. The United States and Canada agreed on a new system of wildlife conservation, and out of the destruction of wildlife rose a new way of dealing with wildlife.

Wildlife was restored during the 20th century, a great ecological success story that is — unfortunately — little appreciated. What was the chief beneficiary among the returned wildlife? What else but the white-tailed deer. From possibly as few as a hundred thousand in 1900, deer populations rose into many millions by the end of the millennium. Estimates vary, but most agree that whitetails are far and above the most numerous big-game animal in North America today. The whitetail also has the greatest public appeal. It is currently riding a crest of unequaled abundance and popularity — the once rare, insignificant little deer.

Opposite: Where trees have toppled and their leaves have turned to leaf-hay, whitetails might avidly congregate in groups. Leaves from tree crowns are less toxic than those on low branches.

Below: After a killing frost in early fall, tree leaves might turn into natural ensilage, in which bacteria and fungi turn cellulose fibers into sugars and proteins. This food is tops for whitetails.

CHAPTER 7

What Makes Whitetails Tick?

Security is the first factor that governs deer behavior. Food is secondary, so deer will trade the best food for security. They will make do with near-starvation rations just so they can live without fear of predators. Moreover, they are astute judges of security, choosing the lesser evil, such as residing close to humans and accepting dogs — which are domesticated wolves — just to escape real wolves. They can also judge human behavior and act upon that experience rationally. How well deer accept people depends on the species. Mule deer — but not whitetails — are easily tamed. However, it also depends on circumstances. You can rest assured that deer will gravitate to the least amount of danger.

When meeting predators is unavoidable, whitetails place themselves in a position to minimize contact and foster effective escape. They are great artists on both counts. You can get a fair picture of that by pursuing whitetails on foot within surroundings chosen by the deer. However, that's not enough. You will also learn by studying deer anatomy and habits as well as hunting methods and what they imply by comparing whitetails of different sex, age and region under varying conditions as well as to other deer. You will also learn by viewing whitetails through another hunter's eyes. Soon, a complex pattern of security adaptations emerges, and little wonder for a deer as avidly pursued by so many predators for many millions of years.

When whitetails flee, they maximize speed by choosing unobstructed ground to run on. That's vital! They choose clear trails, or in the absence of trails, tracks made by large animals. They create a network of trails they know intimately. We know this because deer, when freshly introduced to an area, frequently fail to escape dogs although resident deer escape regularly. Deer use their knowledge of escape terrain to their advantage. Living in a well-explored home range is crucial to deer.

Whitetails readily use roads and then dive into cover at a right angle to the flight path. Pursuers are likely to overshoot and lose the deer's track for a while, allowing it to gain distance. Whitetails also use gravity to maximize their speed by running downhill. They are aided by level ground and impeded by broken terrain and hills. Mule deer, by contrast, choose to run uphill and escape greyhounds in broken terrain, but not on the level! It's topsy-turvy compared to whitetails. Mule deer practice totally different escape strategies, despite being closely related to white-tails!

When on a fast run, whitetails go fairly long distances, thereby increasing time between themselves and the pursuing predator. Time enough for the scent left by their hoofs to evaporate significantly, slowing down the pursuing predator even more. This time trick is also practiced by mule and black-tailed deer, but in a different fashion. These deer depart stotting — or making long bounds — while taking off and landing with their hoofs bunched. Therefore, the cluster of scented tracks are far apart. Nor are they necessarily in a straight line. A nose-oriented dog then zigzags, trying to find the next bound, which gives the deer time to escape.

When running, the white-tailed deer is faster than any other North American deer. Top speeds might reach almost 40 mph, though speeds of up to 45 mph are on record. It uses the rotary gallop, and practices the extended and flexed phases of suspension typical of highly evolved cursors.

Running along obstacle-free trails not only guides deer, but more importantly allows a low hoof trajectory over the ground. Therefore, the escaping whitetail wastes little energy on costly body lift, but sticks it into

Below: White-tailed deer are renowned for flagging with their large white tails during flight.

Right: Although whitetails have evolved as fast runners, they also retained their ancestral skills a saltators. They can progress in high bounds. Whitetails need to be versatile for running in deep snow, swamps, shallow water or tall grass.

forward propulsion. This is done by all speedy runners and gives the subjective impression of a smooth run.

The whitetail's choice of unobstructed runways can be observed in several ways. A buck, bedded at the edge of a thicket, will likely emerge and then run off quickly along the edge of the thicket, thus choosing unobstructed ground. A buck I once wounded circled behind me and then ran along my tracks in the snow until it collapsed. The snow obscured trails, but my tracks were clear and large, and where a large creature passes, so can a whitetail!

In southeastern Alberta, the Cyptress Hills rise above the prairie. The bottom of these hills is covered by dense, intertwined wild rose and snowberry bushes up to 3 feet high. Cattle have punched trails through these low, but extensive, widespread scrub patches. To get through them you must follow cow trails. When snow descends on the land, it quickly engulfs these low shrubs and obscures the trails. Whitetails migrate out of the Cyptress Hills onto the bald prairie and form large herds — right in the open! Mule deer, by contrast, stay behind in the hills, which results in a clean, spatial segregation of whitetails and mule deer. Why so? The snow blanket that engulfs the low shrubbery and obscures the trails robs the whitetail of its ability to quickly run away. Whitetails can develop full speed only on the unobstructed prairie where the footing remains hard. Snow is either blown off the land — thus exposing hard ground — or packed down by wind. Mule deer, which escape by stotting, are not so incapacitated as whitetails, and therefore stay behind on the hills.

ONCE ON A FAST RUN, WHITETAILS GO FAIRLY LONG DISTANCES, THEREBY INCREASING TIME BETWEEN THEM- SELVES AND THE PURSUING PREDATOR.

When on a fast run, an escaping whitetail pays attention to its front as well as its rear. It tries to place an obstacle between itself and the pursuer — be it a bush, hill or tree trunk. It breaks visual contact as fast as possible, depriving the pursuer of a target. It does not stop and look back. It might not need to. The whitetail's eyes are a little more narrowly set than a mule deer's, and are thus less oriented for binocular vision. This suggests a whitetail sees behind it a bit better than do mule deer, and thus better knows what happens to the rear when running.

White-tailed deer are expert hiders and might quietly stay put in cover, allowing predators to pass quite close. Fast acceleration from rest is then doubly important. Whitetails must escape quickly without the slightest delay. Therefore, they might start the run by bursting from hiding very close to the predator. If you hide, you need a fast getaway! A hiding whitetail that bursts forth like a pheasant breaking cover startles the predator and gains time. The whitetail departs low over the ground with rapid, short, powerful bounds, while swinging around to get behind shrubs and tree trunks. Acceleration also increases if the deer beds on a little knoll or hillside so it can burst downhill. Getting ahead of wolves by as little as 100 yards tends to discourage the latter. Most chases last only a few minutes and cover less than a mile. However, wolves can also be blood-mind-

ed and pursue a deer for hours. In one recorded case, a chase lasted more than two hours and covered nearly 13 miles.

Research shows that when pursued by hounds, bucks tend to run in a straight line, relying on speed and endurance to discourage the dogs. Does are more likely to depend on various ruses to shake the pursuer, like running into water and follow a water course, or swimming across water. In rare instances, deer might hide in water with only their nose and eyes protruding. Or they will deliberately run among other deer, which might cause the predator to veer off on the wrong track. A third method is to cross the flight track, thus confusing pursuers.

Playing a ruse on a predator means taking a chance, but does are more likely to get away with this because they are faster runners, can accelerate better, and can dive through smaller openings because they aren't encumbered by antlers. Does don't need the massive shoulder, neck and body mass that bucks require to compete in the rut. However, does become

more susceptible when heavy with fawns, just as all deer become susceptible in snow more than 1½ feet deep, or when weakened by malnutrition,
disease, parasites, old age, and bucks by exhaustion and wounding from
the rut. Fawns are also susceptible to predation, which is one evolutionary
reason for the high reproductive potential of deer.

Having run some distance and broken contact with pursuers, the
whitetail halts to reorientate. Does tend to stay within their home range,
whereas bucks might leave their home range temporarily. Escape on bare
ice tends to be counterproductive because deer lose footing and are easily caught by coyotes or wolves. However, on snow-encrusted ice, the
footing might be very good. Such ice surfaces, for instance, are chosen
regularly by caribou so they can maximize running speed.

Although they are excellent, enduring swimmers, whitetails are unlike-
ly to escape determined wolves by swimming. Wolves have enlarged,
webbed paws, and are excellent swimmers. Observers have seen wolves

Above: Whitetails are expert hiders from
the time of birth. This defense, coupled
with quick running, is efficient protection
against predators. If you hide, you need a
fast getaway!

pursue prey in the water and then dismember them while swimming. Still, deer with access to water appear to better survive wolf predation. In South America, white-tailed deer might also shy from water that contains alligators or anacondas.

Although whitetails have evolved as fast runners, they have also retained their ancestral skills as saltators, meaning they can progress in high bounds. Whitetails are versatile, and they need to be when running in deep, loose snow, or through swamps, shallow water or tall grass. However, saltatorial running is costly and tiring because it requires much costly body lift. It cannot be done for long, nor over great distances. Consequently, saltatorial running is normally practiced in conjunction with hiding.

Where do whitetails hide? They hide where they are concealed, but above all, where they can make effective use of their getaway tactics. By bedding high, their scent blows up, and predators passing below cannot smell them. They also bed in cover large enough to allow them to sneak away quietly, which is an alternative to running away. Whitetails can sneak on their belly, which is unusual for big herbivores! Of course, a consorting buck might also sneak up to an estrous female on his belly — a behavior also seen in mountain goats, but not with the whitetail's closest relative, the black-tailed deer. In rare instances, white-tailed deer hide in holes or, more commonly, under tangles of logs and roots.

I have seen elk, but not whitetails, use slow-motion, upright "pussy-footing," where it slowly and silently places its hoofs on the ground, and then pauses to look and listen every few steps. That is advancing in a manner we call still-hunting. I suspect this observational deficit reflects more on me than the whitetail.

THE WHITETAIL'S EYES ARE A LITTLE MORE NARROWLY SET THAN A MULE DEER'S AND ARE THUS LESS ORIENTED FOR BINOCULAR VISION.

Compared to the closely related mule deer, whitetails are fairly timid in confronting small predators, as we discovered in experimental work with both species. Nevertheless, there are enough observations to show that whitetails will attack predators if pressed — including humans — and that such defenses can be successful. Does protecting fawns are the most likely to attack coyotes or foxes. They use their sharp, hard front hoofs as weapons. Whitetails have also been observed lashing out with their hind legs at a predator. One suspects that large-bodied whitetails are more successful at defense than small-bodied ones. Unlike moose or sambar, white-tailed deer do not have a defensive threat resembling those of wolves. That in itself indicates that flight is preferred over fight by whitetails.

Although the whitetail is highly evolved as a speedy runner, its sensory equipment is not that of a cursor. Cursors are specialized to detect predators, day or night, at fairly long distances. Mule deer — with their large ears, noses and widely spaced eyes angled more for binocular vision — fit the requirements, but not whitetails. Even small-bodied black-tailed deer have eyes a shade larger than whitetails. However, blacktails might need such for nocturnal navigation in old-growth coniferous rain forests that are gloomy by day, let alone by night.

At the least, that implies whitetails rely less on long-distance detection of predators than do mule deer. Mule deer, which detect hunters at great distances, might move at once, while whitetails stay hidden until approached closely by the hunter. Whitetails might be perfectly aware of the approaching danger, but choose to stay and let danger pass, or depart only when in imminent danger. Sometimes under windy conditions, the noise of rustling leaves and wind gusts howling in the treetops hinders hearing. Then, whitetails might detect danger only at close quarters. The signal for quick bolting is eye contact. I have seen whitetails, whether bedded or standing coiled for action, depart the instant our eyes met.

Above: White-tailed deer are fast and able runners that maximize speed via an advanced gallop.

Opposite: Although closely related, mule deer and white-tailed deer practice different escape strategies. White-tailed deer, right, have more narrowly set eyes than do mule deer, left. Therefore, they're less oriented for binocular vision.

Eye contact is a powerful signal under undisturbed social conditions for whitetails, and courtesy — and I use the term deliberately as it correctly applies to whitetails — dictates that eyes are averted from companions to keep the peace. In whitetails, a light ring accentuates the eye, an indication that eye contact is important socially. Eye contact is associated with aggression as well as extreme danger from predation! To understand ground-living large mammals — except primates — one must avoid eye contact, whereas primates absolutely depend on such for much of their communication. Eye contact with a predator is thus the last straw for a whitetail, and it bolts!

The gross morphology and placement of the eyes suggests that during their long history, whitetails were neither occupants of dark, gloomy forests, nor of wide open spaces. Their senses are attuned to cover, and their speedy running carries them between dispersed patches of cover. However, that is a landscape characteristic we expect where

megaherbivores dominate the land.

Our color-sensitive primate eyes also preclude us from seeing the world as whitetails do. We evolved highly sensitive to color, which signaled edible fruit, flowers or insects,. We also love greens, which stand for productivity and signaled worthwhile feeding areas. Although studies on color vision in ungulates confirm they do have such, they have different color vision than we do. How different is uncertain for lack of research. Science works best when it can test crisp, "falsifiable" hypotheses, and

Above: Deep snow is difficult for white-tails to handle. As a last resort, they will push trails through deep snow, but plowing through is costly and inefficient in the face of predators.

Left: Antlerless deer or bucks in velvet are likely to use their front hoofs as weapons on one another. Attacking a companion with flailing front hoofs is severe aggression. A deer threatens such action by erecting its head and laying back its ears. Frequently that's all it takes to make the opponent withdraw.

such are lacking. That is, we have not asked the right questions about the whitetail's vision, or for that matter about its other senses. Some potentially useful clues come from the whitetail's body coloration and observations of what it and its predators pay attention to. Shade contrast is clearly important. In general, ruminants have difficulty with shapes, but are highly sensitive to movement, probably more than we are. Shade contrasts enhance motion detection. I wonder if the whitetail's red summer coat is a camouflage based on red/green blindness in predators. At night,

Above: Whitetails bed where they are hidden, but most of all, where they can easily escape. Therefore, they prefer to bed on a knoll, ridge or slope, and use gravity to run faster downhill.

it turns deer black against a black forest edge. Spotting breaks up the otherwise solid body of the fawn and therefore camouflages it.

The whitetail's auditory world is not only overpowered by wind noises, but also by deer-like movements on noisy forest floors. This is evident when a careful still-hunting approach — slow zigzags and pauses — surprises deer in their beds and might attract bucks, or even predators! I was once rushed by three coyotes when still-hunting at dusk in an aspen grove. They surrounded me. All four looked at each other in surprise, but it did not take long for the three little wolves to regain their wits and dash away. As for the sense of smell, it is to us visually oriented humans a puzzle that awaits clever research to clarify the whitetail's scent world.

Why is it that whitetails on Northern ranges are so poorly adapted to escape predators in deep, loose snow? As long as deer yard in deep snow and develop a complex web of runways, they can escape pursuit with reasonable efficiency. However, they become literally sitting ducks when they jump off the runways into deep snow. Now they can be caught by hand! On Northern ranges, whitetails are sensitive to marauding domestic dogs, but not on Southern ranges. How is such a deficit and contradiction possible in what is otherwise a superlative escape artist?

The answer lies in the whitetail's history. Could whitetails have survived in deep snow under the brutal predation pressure of the Pleistocene? Almost certainly not. They would be bottled up in the South along coastal tall-grass marshes. They augmented the trails left by ele-

Above: In early summer, yearlings are dispersed. Although female yearlings eventually return in late summer to their mothers, yearling males move out permanently and wander until they attach to a fraternal group. Such buck groups are inclined to be friendly and tolerant of newcomers.

Opposite: Sparring bucks tend to lock antlers and twist necks. In sparring, there are no losers and winners. Sparring is frequent in fraternal groups, beginning with velvet shedding and lasting until the bucks lose their antlers.

phants and mastodons in the tall grass with trails of their own. That helped them deal with snow, generating the famous yarding response of white-tailed deer. Glacial times, which outnumbered interglacial times 3-to-1, were climatically benign as the fauna and flora of the glacial refugium that is largely the United States today was shielded from Arctic air by towering continental glaciers. During interglacials, like today, whitetails would be confined by severe predation pressure to Southern regions with little snow. Consequently, we expect whitetail fossils to be concentrated in the southeastern and central parts of the continent, which have low snowfalls even today. And that's what the fossil record shows. Wherever the white-tailed deer struggles against deep winter snows, it is thus a relative newcomer, one less adapted to snow.

The post-Pleistocene collapse of the megafauna left the whitetail as one of few survivors. Freed from competition and severe predation, whitetails multiplied and spread northward into areas with deep winter snow. Today, the whitetail's range reaches much farther north and west than it did in the Pleistocene. Its dispersal toward the equator is thus ancient, but its dispersal north toward the Polar Circle is recent. In fact, it happened in the past two decades!

When we were in the Yukon exploring for ecological reserves in the 1970s, we heard of white-tailed deer sightings. Whitetails were then just south of the Yukon. They had entered the Peace River country of northern British Columbia in the early 1960s. They were confirmed above the 60-degree parallel in the Northwest Territories in 1974. They are not far from Alaska now. I have not seen whitetails in the Yukon or Northwest Territories, but I have seen mule deer in the western Yukon. Their ears were shortened and deformed by frost into cauliflower-like structures, vivid evidence of mismatch between a species and evolutionary environments. Colonizing whitetails are, as expected, very large. Despite wolves, coyotes and mountain lions, deep snow is currently no barrier to their dispersal. Whitetails might reach Alaska in a decade!

It might be pertinent to note that peccaries also dispersed northward after megafaunal extinction to occupy areas within the United States where they had not been present for millions of years. Predation and competition from large-bodied, advanced peccaries now extinct probably bottled up the primitive collared peccary in Central America. We thus see that big-game distributions and their ecology today are artificial, a point that challenges not only our conventional wisdom about wildlife, but puts in doubt conservation policies built on "wilderness" and "ecosystems values" — whatever such might be.

COURTESY AND SPORT ARE THUS TWO ATTRIBUTES OF LIFE IN SELFISH HERDS.

Although running and hiding are individual anti-predator adaptations, white-tailed deer also participate in a collective security called the *selfish herd*. It is a widespread adaptation that, just like individual security measures, has had a powerful effect on the shape and behavior of whitetails. Selfish herds form whenever there is a density of deer and

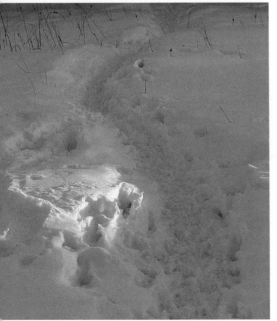

attractive open landscape. We see it in the herds of wintering whitetails on the Montana and Canadian prairies, on the savannas of Texas, in the Llanos of Venezuela, or in modest form wherever whitetails congregate in meadows.

The advantage of a selfish herd is not that more eyes are better at detecting predators, as that does not work at night and is counterbalanced by the increased noise and smells generated by massed deer. The two principal advantages are dilution and positioning. The chance of a deer being singled out by a predator is inversely proportional to the number of deer in a herd. The more deer, the lower the probability of being selected and killed. The chance of being killed is thus "diluted" with increased herd size.

This is greatly enhanced by clever positioning. A deer in the middle of the herd is almost totally safe because a predator is more likely to kill a deer on the periphery. Another position strategy, the *straggler effect*, occurs in flight. In a big herd, the law of averages ensures that some will be slower than others, and predators are likely to zero in on the slowest.

AS LONG AS DEER
YARD UP IN DEEP
SNOW AND DEVELOP
A LARGE, COMPLEX
WEB OF RUNWAYS,
THEY CAN ESCAPE
PURSUIT WITH REA-
SONABLE EFFICIENCY.

Herd members with average running ability are safe indeed, because there will always be laggards for the predators to single out. Consequently, the selfish herd is a poor place for a sick, injured or handicapped deer because any flight will leave it in the rear of the herd. Consequently, we tend to see handicapped deer, including heavily pregnant females, leave the selfish herd and hide.

Within a selfish herd, wounded deer attract predators and are a potential detriment to all. This affects the weapons used in combat, which one can easily determine when comparing species that form selfish herds with ancestral territorial forms. The latter have stiletto-type antlers and horns or combat teeth. These are short, sharp and shaped to penetrate easily as well as slide out easily from the body of an opponent. Such weapons maximize surface damage in fighting, because pain receptors are located just below the skin surface. Consequently, to maximize pain and persuade an opponent to break off the fight and flee, one must wound the body surface.

If you look at the whitetail's genetic twin, the small, territorial brocket deer of South and Central America, you can see the difference. Their antlers are needle-sharp stilettos. To defend against such weapons requires great agility, as in brocket deer, or significant body armor to neutralize the daggers, as in mountain goats or wild boar. However, damaging combat is counterproductive in the selfish herd because it attracts predators. Therefore, there is selection to replace wounding with wrestling, a test of physical strength. In ruminants, this resulted in head-to-head wrestling, in which the antlers or horns are shaped to lock opponents together, allowing full strength wrestling. Short, sharp horns are inadequate for that. Life in the selfish herd leads to the evolution of complex antlers. The primary tasks of complex antlers is thus to lock opponents in combat and protect the bearer against injury. A buck that breaks off an antler is likely to be severely wounded on the side with the missing antler. This type of combat and defense is found in all social horn-bearers, including dinosaurs.

Moreover, life in a selfish herd entails acting in a way that does not spook potential companions, because every companion counts and adds to the safety of the herd. Consequently, we see appeasement behavior freely used, practiced as a courtesy to by small and large alike. In white-tailed deer, this takes the form of walking past companions with head lowered and nose extended while performing a slight crouch. It also entails avoiding eye contact. The calm, uneventful feeding of a large group of whitetails is largely the consequence of courtesy freely extended toward one another. Courtesy used as lubricant in daily affairs is not limited to wise humans. In white-tailed deer, it may be noted, members of buck groups might not only be courteous, but might even show signs of affection such as mutual grooming. This, of course, fosters cohesion and thus adds to the protection of the herd.

With all the potential companions within the selfish herd, there is great opportunity for a complex social life to develop. Associated with complex antlers is a new form of behavior: the sporting, non-injuri-

Below Left: White-tailed deer readily take to water, be they pursued by predators or not. Moving against the current disperses the deer's scent and confuses followers. This species is a superlative disperser that readily crosses large water bodies.

Below Right: Despite their excellent jumping abilities and the high cost of jumping, white-tailed deer nevertheless display great endurance when hunted with dogs. This suggests that, even in flight, they conserve energy and keep their wits about them.

Opposite: When whitetails flee, they choose unobstructed ground to run on. The escaping whitetail thus wastes little energy on costly body lift.

ous weapon engagement we call sparring. It is done only by mutual consent. Nobody gains or loses rank, nobody gets hurt, there are no winners or losers. It unites immature and mature males, and it appears to be great fun for all involved. This is virtually a dimension that is lacking in territorial species, which defend material resources within a given space.

Courtesy and sport are thus two attributes of life in the selfish herds. And that's not all. The selfish herd is also a store of experience and knowledge and a mechanism to exchange such between members. New members soon learn what to take seriously and what to ignore. The herd holds migratory traditions and vital information about key elements for survival, such as water holes, mineral licks, escape terrain, and feeding and wintering grounds. A selfish herd contains great opportunities for learning, and thus favors the evolution of better brains. Social life is associated with increased brain size.

CHAPTER 8

Trade-Off and Compromise

A species' biology is based on compromises, and the whitetail is no exception. On average, the whitetail's security adaptations function best at small body size. Whitetails throughout South America, Central America and southern North America — where the species has a long history — are much smaller than the whitetails from northern North America, where they have but a short history. The size of these Southern white-tailed deer is close to that of pronghorns, which appear to compromise between stride length and stride rate to maximize speed. Large body size might be an advantage in fighting or repelling small predators, but it has severe disadvantages and generates handicaps.

Not only are large bucks denied small spaces for hiding or speedy running through thickets because of their antler spread, but they cannot accelerate from a dead rest as quickly as a small deer, even though they might ultimately reach a higher speed and have more endurance. Nor can they dodge and turn as sharply. Moreover, their smaller surface to mass ratio — contrary to widespread belief — is a poor solution to keeping warm in winter. This belief confuses relative and absolute heat loss, meaning the additional energy expenditure to maintain increased body mass doesn't compensate for the savings generated by a reduced surface-to-mass ratio. Moreover, increased body size is not related to thermal regime — the invalid Bergmann's rule — but to dispersal and colonization. Of that later. Whitetails might be able to surmount many problems, but they cannot surmount the laws of physics. Ironically, deer management, which often aims to produce trophy bucks, handicaps bucks and makes them increasingly dysfunctional. We shall turn to that later.

However, a buck's handicaps are surmountable, because mature bucks are about 51 percent heavier than does. For those who love computing, the exact equation is $y = 9.90 + 0.552x$, $n = 10$, where y = female weight in kg, x = male weight in kg and n = the number of data sets compared. This puts whitetails in the middle of the deer pack. Nevertheless, this tells us that in the whitetail's overall biology, larger size is an important adaptation of males, and smaller males sire fewer offsprings. However, note: By the same token, this suggests big bucks also sire fewer offspring! The most successful bucks are, of course, average. Average is beautiful, literally!

Nevertheless, because mathematical equations are so impressive — the opiate of humdrum science — they must always be regarded with skepticism. For instance, what does one do with the following: Reindeer and caribou in Arctic deserts are small, and males weigh only 20 percent to 40 percent more than females. On productive tundra farther south, barren-ground caribou are bigger, and full grown males are 60 percent to 70 percent heavier than females. In Norway, where reindeer were released from human hands and allowed to roam free of harassment — by humans or predators! — fully grown bulls were 234 percent heavier than females! Under stress and poor feeding conditions, males shrink in size relative to females. Conversely, if you want to grow trophy stags, provide excellent food and ensure there is no harassment by humans or predators. That happens to be part of the century-old formula of European red deer managers who managed for enormous trophy stags. Consequently, the formula, which calculates so precisely the sexual dimorphism of white-tailed deer, is valid only within the bounds and conditions of the data collected. It is a guide, not gospel, and to treat it as such would be a case of misplaced confidence. Although we can reasonably expect that in most natural populations mature white-tailed bucks will weigh 20 percent to 60 percent more than females, we have been warned that given favorable conditions bucks will grow far larger than that relative to females. Bucks will intrinsically maximize body size. Because the same conclusion was reached using different sets of data and arguments for mountain sheep, we are probably correct accepting males as opportunistic maximizers of body size.

WE KNOW SECURITY IS MORE IMPORTANT THAN FOOD. WHICH SECURITY ADAPTATION, HOWEVER, IS MOST IMPORTANT?

We know security is more important than food. Which security adaptation, however, is most important? Is it running, hiding, jumping or confronting predators? We know from experimental hybridization with mule deer that all of the above are under close genetic control because in hybrids all of the above abilities are wrecked and the hybrid is unable to change it. Hybrids have impaired running gaits and are slower than either parent. They hide inappropriately, hit obstacles in jumping, and approach predators without becoming aggressive. This means the whitetail's security adaptations are innate programs that are subject, at best, to maturation, but not to learning. All are so important that unless the fawn is born with a functional program, it will most likely not survive. There is simply no room for learning when being put to the test by

predators. However, note how running is linked to hiding via acceleration, — the use of runways, jumping and dodging, and time for scent to evaporate in the getaway. Speedy running is the central adaptation, and thus the primary escape strategy.

No whitetail deficient in running is likely to survive severe predation. Consequently, running is likely to factor into the female's choice for breeding. In fact, the courtship of whitetails — virtually based on running — is one means by which suitors that cannot run are excluded by the female. Secondly, does have a peak of running activity about the time of estrus. That is, a lot of bucks are made to follow an estrous doe. Female choice is thus exercised by the female presenting the potential suitors with a handicap: Catch her! It's a test of running, a way to ensure superior running ability for her sons and daughters. Therefore, bucks run into a trade-off: If they are small, they are more capable of keeping up with a female by following

Opposite: Running whitetails do not always flag their big tails. Bucks in particular might escape with their tails lowered. This minimizes a predator's ability to detect fleeing prey.

SPEEDY RUNNING IS
HERE THE CENTRAL
ADAPTATION, AND
THUS THE PRIMARY
ESCAPE STRATEGY.

her through the obstacle course she chooses. A large buck might lag, but he will drive off smaller bucks before the competitors can breed. The compromise is between speed and strength, which apparently favors bucks that are about 50 percent or more heavier than does.

To reach a body size at which a buck can successfully contest other bucks, he requires more and better food than the doe. He must maximize food intake. The doe, however, must only optimize food intake, never

maximize. A young female, pregnant with a single fawn, would run the risk of dyctocia if she maximized food intake. That is, she would likely bear a fawn too large to pass her narrow birth canal without damage. She must bear a fawn of optimum, not maximum birth weight. Fawns that are too large might not be born and thus kill the female, or be so damaged that they die, or cause so much pain that the doe deserts them.

Moreover, whitetail females need not bear large young, as even small young are successful hiders, the most common form of securing newborns against predators among deer. It's a different story where the young are born on an open plain in view of predators. Here, babies need to be huge and quick enough to follow their mothers in flight. African wildebeest calves can run at 40 mph within 10 minutes of birth. In the open plain they cannot hide. Whitetail fawns are safe as long as they stay hidden. Only when they begin following their mothers does mortality increase. So, a doe needs to bear only a relatively small child, and she can take some time to grow it to survivable size where it can run right along with her. She does not need to bear huge fawns. In fact, even when loaded down with twins, a doe's relative fetal mass at birth is considerably less than that of a wildebeest female carrying a single calf.

The female can thus emphasize security for her fawn at the expense of food, while the buck can emphasize food over security because he is better adapted at escaping predators than is a fawn. To protect her fawns, the doe only needs a small home range that she knows in detail. The male can roam over a wider area, exploit better food sources and take a few chances with predators. Furthermore, by staying on a small area, the female uses it intensely. We expect the female to rapidly deplete the quality of available

food. That, of course, makes the female's home range unsuitable for raising sons beyond the yearling age. To maximize her fitness, the mother ought to drive off sons from her home range, forcing them to look for better food elsewhere — preferably where other bucks have found good pastures. Only then will her sons have a chance to grow large and competitive. The same does not apply for daughters. In fact, having demonstrated via a high reproductive rate the superior quality of her home range, the experi-

Top: White-tailed deer are classic hiders that spend the first weeks of life in seclusion. Fawns are masters at hiding, and might be aided in camouflage by the many light spots on their fur that — to a predator's eyes — break up their shape.

Bottom: Whitetails are experts at hiding — and at sprinting away — if detected by a predator.

enced, competent mother might leave her home range to her daughters and set up shop elsewhere!

The above compromises generate an ecological segregation of sexes for most of the year. It minimizes competition for food, to which white-tailed deer are exceptionally sensitive, and probably fosters superior reproduction and survival of all. It is likely that at high population densities this segregation and all its benefits will break down. But then, throughout their

Above: The bond between mother and fawn is close. However, in the first weeks of life, mother visits baby but a few times a day. After lengthy suckling and cleaning, the fawn moves off to hide again.

Opposite: Related whitetails engage in much mutual grooming. This can continue for years among mother and daughter.

long history under severe predation pressure it might well be that whitetails did not need mechanisms to deal with crowding.

Yearling bucks that are kicked out by their mothers need to find superior feeding areas soon. They disperse and explore, or better still, find other bucks and adopt their successful way of life. The fraternization of bucks, so conspicuous in whitetails, arises as a consequence of young males attaching themselves to older bucks, probably using them as a lead to superior feeding and security. Now the sparring ceremony comes into its own. It is profoundly different in white-tailed deer than in almost all other deer, except the closely related mule deer. Young males appear to go out of their way in befriending older bucks and creating strong bonds. They do this via sparring, which is a sporting, friendly antler engagement in which there is no contest and no winners or losers.

The start of a sparring relationship can be elaborate and eye-catching. A young buck starts to look toward a large one, who feeds on, ignoring the young one. The latter approaches cautiously, still looking at the bigger buck. Then the young one lowers himself, extends its head and neck just above the ground and crawls to the big buck's rear. It sniffs the urine-strained tarsal glands of the big fellow — who continues feeding. Such feeding among gazelles, antelope and deer is a peace signal. Now the young buck crawls around the big fellow and, still crouching, faces him. The little buck begins to lick the large buck's face, who has paused and is holding still. As the young buck proceeds with licking the face, it licks further up, on the forehead. Now it rises from the crouch, gently angles its antlers forward and makes antler contact with the big buck. Sparring commences.

In sparring, the bucks rely initially on fairly gentle neck-twisting. There is no pushing and shoving, although such might occur after the bucks know one another when they are regular sparring partners. Then, minor liberties might be taken. Normally, the smaller engages and disengages. However, this rule is violated after bucks befriend and are on sparring terms. Sparring becomes more vigorous among acquainted bucks. No matter how long or vigorous, in a sparring match the bigger buck acts dominantly. In elk and other Old World deer, sparring partners assume both roles: They act symmetrically. Whitetails assume asymmetrical roles in sparring. Serious fights look quite different from sparring engagements. Fights are a last-ditch effort to settle rank and access to females. Fighting has nothing to do with sparring. In fact, fights segregate bucks instead of bonding them.

Because it is so complex and frequently practiced, we are justified in concluding that membership in a fraternal group confers significant benefits to a young buck. However, we still have much to learn about fraternal groups. They form, as in the related mule deer, right after the rut and continue in some fashion till the following rut. Fraternal groups are larger and more likely where whitetails are common and there is much open country. They are smaller and rare among whitetails from dense forests. After antler shedding, bucks show up in female groups and are difficult to tell from does. It might be that bucks find some protection from predation by looking like females in a female herd between antler shedding and antler regrowth. Not to be conspicuous to predators in a selfish herd is important!

SEGREGATION OF THE SEXES PROBABLY FOSTERS SUPERIOR REPRODUCTION AND SURVIVAL OF ALL.

CHAPTER 9

To the Ends
of the Earth

A myth surrounding whitetails is that they are unspecialized generalists. This misconception arises from the whitetail's rather primitive teeth, a sign they are not adapted to abrasive foods such as coarse grasses, and dust- and grit-covered herbs. Their teeth have actually enlarged a little since they appeared nearly 4 million years ago, a sign that they adapted to savannah and grasses. In South America, whitetails inhabiting extensive grasslands show even more plains adaptations by having larger teeth as well as larger antlers and tails. Ditto for our little "flagtail" from Arizona, the Couse deer. Yes, life in the open affects the configuration of the front and rear end of deer. It visually enhances the anterior and posterior probably for better signaling over greater distances.

Unspecialized teeth are actually the hallmark of most deer. The big bamboo-eating sambar of southeastern Asia, which is almost as large as an elk and resembles one as well, is one exception. Its cheek teeth are elongated. To a lesser extent, so are the same teeth of the beautiful axis deer of India and Ceylon, a gregarious grass grazer. Deer have been loath to become grass feeders and thus increase the size and complexity of their teeth and gut. Deer greatly depend on the higher protein and mineral content of dicotyledonous plants to supply the high demands of antler growth. Grasses simply do not cut it as food for growing antlers. Forbs and foliage do! It is, therefore, correct not to characterize the white-tailed deer as a grazer. However, this does not mean the whitetail is not specialized. He is! And highly specialized at that, but for a different purpose. Whitetails are specialized as dispersers and colonizers. Please note this is the exact opposite of a food-competitor. Whitetails have been shaped by nature not to go head-to-head against competitors over deteriorating food supplies. Instead, they pull stakes and excel at quickly finding a better place to live and colonize.

One legacy of the severe predation whitetails endured for millions of years is that they require high-quality food to thrive. That was also true of its fellow travelers. Native North American herbivores were huge compared to Eurasian counterparts, but equipped with simpler and smaller

TO THE ENDS OF THE EARTH **109**

Above: Lush, blooming meadows and open hillsides, like this one in Wisconsin, offer highly digestible, nutrient-rich vegetation. Whitetails are sure to find and exploit such areas, particularly when lactating, depositing fat and growing hair or antlers.

teeth. This suggests American megaherbivores were predator-limited, but Eurasians were food-limited. That is, because of severe predation in North America, vegetation was less severely cropped and high-quality food was generally in good supply. If it had not been, Colombian mammoths and long-horned bison would have evolved much larger and complex teeth as they ground out more nourishment from increasingly poorer forage. That's what their counterparts, the woolly mammoth and steppe wisent, did in Eurasia. Thus, when mammoths and bison came to North America from Siberia, they had rather primitive teeth. Their Siberian relatives, sub-

ONE LEGACY OF THE
SEVERE PREDATION
WHITETAILS
ENDURED FOR
MILLIONS OF YEARS
IS THAT THEY
REQUIRE HIGH-
QUALITY FOOD TO
THRIVE.

sequently, evolved more complex teeth as they filled habitats to carrying capacity and were forced to deal with crowding and depleted food resources. Because grazers select the best food at any time, their collective grazing progressively reduces the quality of their food, causing the remaining plants to develop increasingly tougher fibers. To get value out of tough fibers, fine grinding is needed so it can be better digested. That job falls to increasingly larger teeth with more complex chewing surfaces. Living on more fibrous, more difficult-to-digest food led not only to larger and more complex teeth, but also to smaller body size. Conversely, mammoths and long-horned bison arriving in North America were under severe predation pressure. Because the number of prey was kept low by sophisticated predators, there was more high-quality, less-fibrous food available. This did not require larger and more complex teeth than they already had. It did require, however, better abilities to escape predators and larger body sizes to successfully confront predators. Luxurious feeding conditions promoted large body size anyway. Consequently, after parting company, mammoths and long-horned bison in Eurasia became smaller, but evolved larger and more complex teeth. Meanwhile, the brethren they parted with in North America grew ever bigger in body size and acquired sophisticated anti-predator adaptations, but their teeth remained small and primitive because of the high-quality food they lived on.

This story repeats itself with other species. For instance, primitive moose entered North America from Siberia in mid-Pleistocene times. Moose that stayed in Siberia continued specializing their nose as an instrument of aquatic feeding, evolving the famous "moose nose," which was a response to food shortage. Moose that had crossed into North America with the simpler nose changed in the face of severe predation, but retained the primitive nose. Therefore, it had a more deer-like face. That was the American stag moose *Cervalces*. It is extinct and has been replaced postglacially by another wave of moose — advanced moose with the funny "moose nose" that came from Siberian to Alaska about 10,000 years ago.

Although Ice Age North America was a dangerous place to life and extracted severe anti-predator adaptations from prey species, it must have had high-quality food in abundance. The white-tailed deer depends on such and moves when food becomes poor. We expect, therefore, that it is a poor food competitor that cannot stand competition for food.

Below and Right: In early fall, acorn mast is a vital deer food that is avidly searched out by deer of all ages. A good acorn crop ensures a good deposit of fat for bucks and does. Bucks use fat deposits during the rut, and does use it to support gestation.

Therefore, if placed with Eurasian deer that evolved as a food-limited species, white-tailed deer are expected to do poorly and even go extinct. White-tailed deer introduced to New Zealand have done poorly in the presence of European red deer. So have introduced mule deer. White-tailed deer did not take a foothold in Europe except on agricultural lands in Finland in the absence of roe or red deer. The obverse situation — introducing Eurasian deer on white-tailed deer ranges — also produced the expected results. White-tailed deer declined or went extinct in the presence of foreign competitors.

Although successful throughout the Americas, whitetails cannot colonize to the ends of the Earth because they will be stopped by better food competitors. And there are plenty! That's important to remember when managing for white-tailed deer:

They can be readily out-competed by superior food competitors. That's the great weakness of the white-tailed deer.

Whitetails thus choose luxury and the thrills and uncertainties of dispersal and colonization over the drudgery and pain of stodgy competition for ever poorer food. This is a deer designed by nature not to compete, but to disperse, search for and exploit rich food sources. Though it has a rumen like sheep, a whitetail's is smaller and passes digested food rapidly. This deer is an adventurer! Rich forage is, invariably, associated with dis-

LUXURY FOOD PROMOTES NOT ONLY LARGE BABIES AND PLENTY OF MILK. IT ALSO CHANGES THE FAWNS FUNDAMENTALLY.

turbed sites and ecological rejuvenation. Early, productive ecological successions follow fire, floods, wind storms, avalanches or megaherbivores — wherever vegetation has been set back. In modern times, we can add agriculture, forestry, recreation, transportation and suburbs as destructive agents that, inadvertently, provide the whitetail with high-quality food. Thus, the more disturbance, the more deer.

The richer and more diverse the forage, the bigger the bodies and the larger the antlers. Farm fields of corn, alfalfa and winter wheat, fertilized lawns, parks, gardens and orchards all attract deer. And so do the real carriers of fertility and power: floods. Rivers fed by streams that carry fertile silt from glaciers, which bring masses of drift ice, annually scour and plow the flood plain and set back vegetation to early seral stages. Fertility, pioneering plants and vigorous growth are concentrated, making such rivers great whitetail habitat. Whitetails in abundance always speak of ecological havoc, fertile lands and young ecosystems.

Dispersal as a grand strategy begins with hunger. As food supplies run down, it gets tougher or more dangerous to get. The whitetail pulls stakes and is off, even without food depletion. Successful adult females might leave their home ranges for their daughters and granddaughters. These matriarchs challenge fate by searching for unoccupied places to start a new home and matriarchy. They must have either a better chance at success than their inexperienced daughters, or ensure superior reproductive success for their stay-at-home daughters for this type of dispersal to have evolved. Which of the alternatives is valid, we do not know. Sacrificing oneself for one's children is hardly unheard of in the living world, being the essence of altruism. Is the whitetail matriarch's gamble altruistic or opportunistic? After all, she might simply switch selfishly to a better site she has discovered in her roaming.

A whitetail's high birthrate and the exceedingly rapid maturation of female fawns leads to rapid colonization and rapid exploitation of available food. Luxury food promotes large babies and plenty of milk, and changes fawns fundamentally. This is a universal change, one that promotes better dispersal and colonization — believe it or not — even in humans. Collective findings suggest that high-protein, prenatal nutrition allows offspring to be livelier, more inquisitive, more clever, more playful, harder to discourage, less-easily frightened, more independent, as well as larger and healthier. These are attributes needed by a disperser and colonizer to deal with novel opportunities and dangers.

Poor prenatal nutrition produces the obverse, namely, tenacious, frugal, long-lived, stay-at-home types reluctant to innovate or leave! So whenever whitetails are dispersing and colonizing new land, expect large body

Below: Fawns might act like adults and even indulge occasionally in sparring matches. They follow the same rules as adult bucks.

size, as well as lively but sensitive individuals. Where whitetails hang on under poor conditions, expect tough little deer. Where whitetails colonize, expect high reproduction and early maturation. Where they are small, expect few fawns and late maturation. These different versions of deer are called dispersal, or giant, and maintenance, or dwarf, phenotypes. The differences are not in genetics, but in the expressions of genetic potential. It takes about five generations on good food to turn maintenance into dispersal phenotypes. One is not better than the other. Both are adaptive responses of the genome, one fitting conditions of luxury, the other of poverty. A buck grown under luxury conditions will not pass on larger antlers to his sons any more than a buck grown under conditions of poverty will pass on smaller antlers to its off-spring.

Whitetails, in addition to rapidly changing to a dispersal form, have a high capacity for reproduction, and for dispersing as year-lings before reproduction and even as adults after reproduction. Whitetails roam widely, even living as drifters with no fixed home range in wide open spaces. They take readily to water and are excellent swimmers. These are all attributes of a disperser.

Now we add process and time to colonization and see that whitetails — upon finding a source of high-quality food — change rapidly into large-bodied dispersing whitetails. This lasts as long as the food lasts. In fertile river valleys and deltas, which are fertilized and rejuvenated annually by silt-laden floods, this is a perpetual process. In burned forests, which revert to climax forests, this process is limited to early stages in the ecological progression. When food becomes scarce, whitetails revert to smaller body size, delayed maturation and reduced reproduction, but they hang on. When food conditions are too poor, they go extinct. Although they are still hanging on, no wandering whitetails will compete with them, because the poor food makes them move on. A severe winter might exterminate the population until another forest fire sets back the ecological successions.

The change from dispersal giants to maintenance dwarfs burns up available food to generate more whitetails that wander off in search of more food to burn up. And so it goes. This pattern is not unfamiliar to students of rodent populations, especially mouse plagues. Good food spots or good years are used to crank out lots of bodies to saturate the landscape, ensuring that resources within reach are eaten by dispersers while the home folks hang on! It's a dynamic system to ensure that unpredictable food resources are found and used at the cost of losing a significant number of dispersers to failure. Lightning-set fires are the foremost unpredictable agent of habitat generation. When habitat patches are fixed, as are mountain grasslands, a different system of habitat retention evolves: the close association of adults and young to transmit home range knowledge as a tradition. Mountain sheep practice such intensely so that sheep biology is

IN MODERN TIMES, WE CAN ADD AGRI-CULTURE, FORESTRY, RECREATION AND SUBURBS AS DESTRUCTIVE AGENTS THAT INADVERTENTLY PROVIDE HIGH-QUALITY FOOD.

utterly subservient to that tradition. However, knowledge of seasonal home ranges is also passed from generation to generation by white-tailed deer, mother to daughter and granddaughter within the maternal clan, and from old buck to young buck in fraternal groups. However, whitetails are flexible! They move readily on and off ranges depending on snowfall, blizzards or green-up as well as their own body condition. Fat whitetails seek wintering yards least and latest! Mountain sheep have rather firm, chronological movement patterns, but whitetails move opportunely with circumstances.

Body size varies locally with food conditions, independent of genetics. Also, body size is largest where whitetails have started to colonize. In addition, it varies in a peculiar fashion with latitude. Our big-game animals increase in body size with latitude to about the 60th parallel north, but then reverse and decrease in size sharply. Thus body size is smallest at

Below: In the West, whitetails — often in groups — readily move onto the prairie to feed. The smallest units are matriarchal groups, but these readily join one another in "selfish herds." These deer feed less on grasses than on herbs and the foliage and fruits of low shrubs, such as prairie rose and snow berry.

low and again at high latitudes. For species that do not reach 60 degrees north, Bergmann's Rule has been invoked as an explanation, stating that size increases to combat heat loss through a reduction in the surface-to-mass ratio. The rapid decline in body size of species north of 60 degrees north has not been taken into account. If whitetails followed Bergmann's Rule and compensated cooling by growing large, they would quickly bloat to the size of elephants and beyond!

Growing large is a poor way to keep warm. The absolute energy costs in growing large far outweigh the small savings in energy derived from a smaller surface-to-mass ratio. Based on empirical evidence only, we expect whitetails to reach maximum size — all other factors being equal — at about 60 degrees north or at the altitudinal equivalent. That is, because altitude and latitude compensate for one another, we expect an increase in body size in whitetails with altitude and then a reversal at high altitudes. This has not been documented for whitetails, but has been documented

for roe deer in the European Alps. The turning point in altitudinal body size, so theory predicts, is the elevational equivalent of 60 degrees north. We have no data for whitetails, but it sure works for bighorns!

What are the causes for latitudinal/altitudinal size changes? They are nutrition. Summer brings a surplus of food. At high latitudes, summer productivity is high but too short to allow full body growth. In hot climates, the surplus productivity of summer is also too short for full body growth. At about 60 degrees north, productivity is high and summers are long enough for animals to enjoy the longest "vacation from want."

Dwarfs? The smallest whitetails are in forested tropics and islands. Why? In the tropics, essential nutrients are not bound up in soils as much as in living tissues. These are severely defended by the host against myriad predators, parasites and pathogens. Because of stable climatic conditions, few opportunities exist to exploit a windfall of food, such as deer experience in summer in Northern latitudes. Competition is relentless and

high-quality food is continually in short supply, which constrains body growth.

Islands normally have a marine climate that dampens temperature oscillations and precludes high swings in food availability. That encourages populations to build up and closely crop available food so that even in summer there is little relief from want and competition. Too many mouths set back the vegetation and even shorten the productivity pulse, should there be one. Islands might also experience lower biodiversity in plants, and thus fewer species to forage on. Yet diversity of food enhances digestibility. Lower food variability also lowers body size. Moreover, mild maritime climates might not allow vegetation to freeze, thereby preventing the killing and subsequent detoxification of forbs as well as natural ensilage formation. Fibrous, poisonous green forage is hard to digest and thus, counterproductive for body growth. Consequently, island forms are normally smaller than mainland forms.

Finally, island forms isolated from predators for millennia on end grow tiny as a consequence of being able to reproduce at ever smaller body sizes, which can lead to extremes in dwarfism. It's a process that can shrink elephants from 12 feet to 3 feet in shoulder height! In birds, of course, predator-free islands generate giants because depleted biodiversity selects larger eggs and greater adult abilities in the newly hatched. However that's another story. Few island dwarfs or giants have made it into modern times because these helpless creatures were quickly exterminated, directly or indirectly, upon contacts with humans. The Florida Key deer might be the closest we come to an island dwarf in whitetails.

Opposite: White-tailed deer are primarily foliage feeders. Whether dead or alive, foliage tends to be very nutritious, allowing deer access to high-quality forage most of the year. When foliage dies back and falls off, it tends to turn into nutritious natural ensilage, which might be available throughout winter. Another benefit of hardwoods is the production of mast in early fall.

Some scientists have proposed that parasites and pathogens are allies that help a species out-compete invaders. The logic is clear: In an old species, such as the whitetail, parasites and pathogens have reached a dynamic compromise. Parasites have become less virulent because debilitating or killing the host reduces the parasite's chance of survival and reproduction. At the same time, the host has become more resistant to its parasites. Enter a closely related invader. It has little resistance to the parasites and might perish because of this. It's nice theory, too nice to be true!

On the face of it, whitetails do carry many parasites and pathogens, and yes, some can be lethal to other species. Foremost among these are the brain or meningeal worm, the winter tick and the large American liver fluke. Elk, moose and caribou that come in contact with whitetails carrying brain worms are often doomed — the elk being the most resistant of the three. It also suffers less from the whitetail's ticks, which can devastate moose. The giant liver fluke can also be lethal, particularly to livestock. Thus, there is no place for moose and caribou where there are dense whitetailed deer populations carrying these parasites. However, these species are not competitors of whitetails, and although elk might be, it is the least

affected. Moreover, despite these parasites, whitetails decline and even disappear in the presence of sika and other Old World deer. In the West, the brain worm has not kept pace with the whitetail's advance, and Western whitetails do not infect other species with the dreaded brain worm. Here, it is displacing the mule deer but via a different mechanism. Moreover, whitetails have not done well in the face of livestock diseases, such as foot-and-mouth disease, bovine tuberculosis or listeriosis. Whatever benefits co-adapted parasites and pathogens might have for the host, there is plenty of evidence that whitetails do succumb to such, especially in times of stress. Parasites and pathogens are questionable allies to whitetails.

To the ends of the Earth? Whitetails in Alaska? Yes, they are heading that way, and given a bit more global warming and the inevitable forest fires associated with it, whitetails will spread from the Yukon to Alaska. They will be big initially, as long as they are dispersing and living

off the burn's rich vegetation. They will eventually decline, however. Wolves feeding off good moose populations might delay whitetails, but it's not going to be forever. As the boreal forest in Canada burns or is depleted by logging, whitetails will move in and flourish. They are expanding in the West and are displacing mule deer. We expect the latter to survive in small pockets of steep terrain such as sandhills and badlands. Where private over public interests dominate, whitetails will likely be managed for trophy bucks, and their genes mixed with others from distant areas in the vain hope of improving trophy size. Where human populations burgeon in their Southern distribution, whitetails will be increasingly confined to protected areas, with many populations going extinct. However, let the human population problem flag, and they will be right there, exploiting the return of vegetation to the scarred earth. That is their strength. They are great colonizers. Whatever the havoc, whitetails will know how to exploit it. They will be with us for a while!

WHATEVER THE HAVOC, WHITETAILS WILL KNOW HOW TO EXPLOIT IT. THEY WILL BE WITH US FOR A WHILE!

CHAPTER 10

The Whitetail's Art

It happened a good many years ago, but the scar on my friend's hand still tells of his close call. At the time, he was a young, energetic warden at a zoo, who looked after whitetails in a large paddock. He was inside the paddock when a buck approached. Suddenly, the buck charged and pinned my friend against the fence. Fortunately, the antlers surrounded my friend's belly. He had put up his hands to catch the antlers and now tried to hang on for dear life. In the process, an antler tine punctured his hand. My friend got out.

What happened here — an unprovoked and unpredictable attack by a male ungulate — has happened many times in zoos, sometimes with more tragic consequences. In that zoo, two wardens were sent to the hospital by elk and mountain goats, and each story is similar to the one above. I visit zoos and hear this story repeated a good many times. It is followed by the admonition that one has to be careful. However, I have never heard anyone state the correct solution to this problem: Learn the body language of the deer! None of the deer, elk or mountain goats failed to signal its intentions.

After four decades of study, I can state categorically that there are no "unpredictable" attacks. There is, nevertheless, a deep, fundamental problem, that resides within us: We do not instinctively understand the most serious of threats signaled by male deer or other male ungulates. This applies not merely to Joe Average, but to observant, intelligent people working closely with large herbivores, including scientists with degrees in animal behavior. I cringe at how often I see tourists in national parks walk toward an elk that is telling them to get lost just to have their picture taken — sometimes with child in arm and their backs to the elk. Yellowstone National Park is the center for bison attacking tourists. Tourists walk up to a bull from the side, and before they can pet the woolly head, they have the bull's horn in their body. How is it possible? The bull was only standing there. Forget the warden service in that institution as a source of helpful information. In preparation for a lawsuit, I found their understanding of basic big-game behavior wanting in the extreme — with no remedy in sight. And that is as unfortunate as it is needless. So, let's get to the basics of white-tailed deer communication, beginning with fundamentals.

You and I have a severe handicap in interpreting a deer's body language. Remember the Big Bang that terminated dinosaurs and spread tall forests from coast to coast? Remember that it split mammals into two ecological factions, one that lived in trees and the other that stuck to the ground? We belong to the faction that went into the trees, and whitetails belong to the faction that stayed on the ground. In the trees, there is plenty of light, and communication soon centered on vision and voice. When two communicate in a tree at close quarters, they are likely sitting on the same branch and must communicate eye-to-eye, face-to-face, chest-to-chest.

Opposite: Bucks in fraternal groups are on good terms and might groom before sparring. Such grooming is initiated by the subordinate.

Below: A rare, all-out dominance fight between matched bucks. The force of the attack is caught by the defending buck's antlers (left). The attacking buck tries to force the defending buck backward. Antlers not only guard against attacks, but also permit locking of heads in all-out wrestling engagements. The buck on the right was the winner.

OPPONENTS
ADDRESSING ONE
ANOTHER LOOK PAST
EACH OTHER.
LOOKING DIRECTLY
AT AN OPPONENT
EITHER SIGNALS OR
SQUELCHES AN
ATTACK.

The two communicators look at each other. If one faces away, its rear pole is placed prominently before the other. The two body parts seen predominantly are face and chest and the rear. This is where primates center their decorations that aid in communication. We expect — instinctively! — eye-to-eye contact if and when we communicate.

The whitetail's ancestors stayed on the dusky, gloomy forest floor. Here they carried on with the ancient vertebrate signaling system, based on four-legged animals moving about on a flat floor while playing up body size to impress each other. Eye-to-eye contact was suppressed. Therefore, opponents looked past each other. Looking directly at an opponent either signals an attack or — performed by a subordinate — squelches an attack. The presence of a mask enhances the stare signal. Visual signals were augmented by strong olfactory signals, particularly for night use, and vocal signals were suppressed for security reasons.

A white-tailed buck, testing an opponent, moves at a tangent toward the opponent —never directly at him. He is performing the first motions in a dominance display. He looks away from the opponent. He does it pointedly! Unless in deep grass, he will keep his head low.

Let's hold it here for a moment: If a tame buck angles in your direction with eyes averted, get out at once. You have no time to lose. You are in imminent danger of being attacked.

As the buck advances, he raises the body hair all over his body — a little at first, making him appear darker. He lays his ears back. He opens up his tarsal gland brushes. The bigger the buck, the more he has urinated on those tarsal brushes and the smellier he is. This particular scent is his personal signature, which he is now wafting about. He lifts up his tail, but keeps it curved downward, thereby enlarging his body. He walks slowly and stiffly, as if a bit muscle-bound. As he approaches and further raises his hair, he opens his small preorbital glands. The little white metatarsal gland low on the hind legs might also be flared.

A buck advancing in this fashion signals with his angle of approach. He uses a distinct body posture, noticeable through the position of his head, ears, hair, tail and glands and his slow motion. He has started a dominance display, a challenge toward an opponent or possibly toward you. Superficially, it looks like he is merely sauntering closer. After all, if you are his target, he is not directly addressing you — though he is addressing you! His approach is indirect. Unless you are specifically aware of what

Opposite: Antler punctures can lead to infections and pus formation, as is the case here. Rutting bucks sustain 30 to 50 antler punctures per season, and must heal from the damage inflicted as well as the infections caused by deep inoculation with dirty tines.

Below: Some rutting bucks do not survive the rut — casualties of vicious combat. Most wounds are found on the head, neck and haunches. Occasionally necks are broken or the skull and body are deeply penetrated by tines.

Above: A courting buck is likely to run in a low stretch after a female. Normally, an estrous white-tailed doe leads a buck on long, severe runs. This might be a test of the male's running ability and its endurance. Both of which are vital in escaping predators.

he is doing, you might overlook this. If a buck approaches in such a fashion, you are in mortal danger. Get away!

Why is a dominance display by a buck so dangerous? Let's continue watching. If the buck approaches another buck in dominance display, the smaller one will raise its head and deliberately stare at the approaching dominant. Note: When a whitetail stares at you, it is most noticeable. The stare is sharply accentuated by the light rings around its eyes, its black nose, its light ears often rimmed with black and its white throat patch, which is especially prominent in bucks. The subordinate will evade the advance at a dis-

tance, circling to the dominant's rear. He will not allow the dominant to come too close. He will also depress hair and tail, and thus
look sleek, light, small and short. He will raise his head high, but
depress his back while the dominant's back tends to be slightly
arched. A buck is likely to attack if the opponent is close, and if he
does not pay attention. A dominant will not rush heedlessly into an
attack, but will do so opportunistically. He uses the element of surprise. By keeping at a distance and by deliberately staring at the
dominant, the subordinate signals that it will not be surprised. If,
as my friend did, one ignores an approaching buck in dominance

display, the buck is not held back by eye contact, and is quite likely to attack because the opponent is not looking. Also, large bucks will charge small ones without too many niceties of dominance display. We can infer from this that a buck hesitates to attack an opponent he slightly fears. If the subordinate evades the displaying dominant, the latter might follow and snort or grunt, rubbing in his victory. More likely than not, the lesser will begin feeding, a peace signal among bovids and cervids, and the larger will join in.

If the buck being displayed to is similar in body and antler size, it might display back in kind. Now the dominance displays escalate as the bucks begin circling one another. Neither looks at the other, except by sneaking a quick glance. That might look deceptively like a showy twisting of antlers for the benefit of the opponent. That's questionable, because antler displays closely follow courtship structure, but not displays toward other males. Eye aversion and keeping close track of the opponent are in conflict, hence the periodic quick check on the opponent. The motions become stiff, the tarsal glands are extremely flared, as are the preorbital glands. One or the other might break off the display to shred a bush or paw the ground. If the displays continue, both might crouch — unless in deep grass — and really slow down. This is preparation against a surprise attack, depriving the opponent of a target while getting set to catch the expected rush of antlers. It might not come to that, as one buck might suddenly bolt and trigger a quick chase by the other.

If neither gives way, the bucks might make little motions with the antlers that betray their readiness to catch the attack. It comes with lightning speed and incredible force. Such dominance fights however, are rare. Dominance displays are a way of testing the nerves of other bucks, minimizing overt aggression that is damaging and costly. In fact, it tends to be costly to both opponents, which makes it imperative to minimize fighting. The alternative is psychological warfare, appearing large through erect body and hair, confident by dispersing scent from the tarsal gland, and brave by making a racket shredding a bush or vocalizing. Deer normally avoid this so as not to attract predators.

But why the tangential, indirect approach or the sidling? Why the eye aversion? Let's return to basics: What is the goal of a dominance display? It is to cow an opponent and to make him give up without a contest. It aims at achieving at a low cost what otherwise would be achieved by expensive fighting. An indirect approach deprives the opponent of predictability, which our innate systems oppose. Why not keep the opponent there? Keep advancing indirectly while enlarging apparent body size. Size is fundamentally important in winning fights. It's a factor opponents must be sensi-

Upper Left: A severely horned sapling, a sign that a brave and probably large buck was at work here.

Upper Right: Old, bold and dominant bucks will likely rub large trees, gouging them severely with their sharp and rugose brow tines. Other roaming bucks will horn the same spot, marking over the scent of the preceding buck.

Bottom Left: Central to the marking behavior of white-tailed deer are overhead limbs that bucks cover with scent, including secretions from preorbital glands, as shown here. Bucks also chew and lick such limbs, rub them with their frontal glands, and thrash them with their antlers.

Bottom Right: Urine runs in a thin stream into the long hair of the tarsal glands, which are also called tarsal brushes. From there, it drips into the scrape, soaking into the well-worked, absorbent mineral soil. A female looking for a specific mate can link the scrape to a buck. Females sometimes urinate near the scrape.

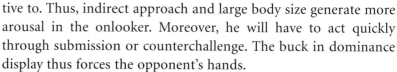

THE WHITE-TAILED
BUCK EXTENDS HIS
PERSONALITY WELL
BEYOND HIS BODY.
WHITETAILS
PRIMARILY USE
SCENT TO SPREAD
THEIR PRESENCE
OVER A LARGE AREA.

tive to. Thus, indirect approach and large body size generate more arousal in the onlooker. Moreover, he will have to act quickly through submission or counterchallenge. The buck in dominance display thus forces the opponent's hands.

Why does the dominant buck avoid eye contact? Eye contact signals intention. Eye contact is made by dominants about to charge at a hopelessly inferior buck. Or, it is made before flail-fights with front legs, which bucks in polished antlers do not indulge in. Or, it is a sign of potential submission by a buck afraid of the dominant. In human terms, the pointed aversion of eyes is like saying, "I am deliberately ignoring you." That, of course, has a human counterpart between unfriendly close acquaintances. Eye aversion at close range is an assertion of superiority by the dominant. A confident buck does not have to look at another!

It is a good practice to sketch dominance displays of various mammals, because it forces you to look closely at the animal's body. When sketching, one notices small details and the arrangement of body parts and motions. If you also have some acquaintance with classical art and how to construct picture planes, a study of dominance displays leads to a surprising revelation. A buck in full dominance display generates a picture plane that follows the rules of classical Occidental art. In the whitetail, it is less obvious than in some other species, such as bison, nilgai, gazelles, oryx antelope, various wild goats and even mule deer. Nevertheless, it is there, as well as optical illusions that augment body size. These combine to make the onlooker's eye flit over the buck's entire displaying body.

The bottom line is that we share basic visual neurophysiological mechanisms with white-tailed deer. In the final analysis that's hardly a big surprise.

The white-tailed buck extends its personality well beyond its body — and so, of course, do we. Whitetails use scent to spread their presence over a large area, with the ultimate purpose of facilitating reproduction and the buck's survival. The urine-impregnated tarsal gland is the buck's signature, the fundamental carrier of chemical messenger molecules called pheromones. The buck's urine is attractive to females, helps bring them into heat, and thereby advances and shortens the mating season. That's to the buck's advantage because a reduction in the length of the rut reduces rutting costs and increases the male's survival. The buck, by skillfully spreading his scent over an area, can in his absence attract females, keeping them excited and close by. By patrolling the markers in his area, a buck can

meet, court and mate more females. Moreover, females harassed by yearling males know where to run for relief.

Old bucks not only keep yearling males in check, but have greater ritual and restraint in their courtship, giving the female some respite from sexual harassment. This wide-flung system of marking might extend several miles, ensuring both sexes meet when whitetails are at a low density — as they probably were during the Pleistocene Period. Such meeting is, of course, facilitated by the bucks dispersing and traveling over large areas. Compared to some Old World deer, the whitetail's rut is a fairly quiet, secretive affair, again suggesting the effects of exceptional predation in the past.

However, all scent-marking is a dominance display. Primarily addressed to females, it is nevertheless noticed by other bucks, which might try to deposit their own discrete scent mark beside it, or cover it with their own scent. This is a universal behavior in large mammals. If one buck paints his scent over a rival's, it can be cause for the original buck to re-scent his earlier mark. That marking is self-assertion, which is evident because a buck, after chasing off a rival, might start marking. It's analogous to a bull elk screaming his bugle after a defeated rival.

Above: A northern Florida buck marks a cypress knee, a portion of the tree's root system protruding from the swamp water. Bucks make use of whatever structure that can serve as a signpost.

Opposite: White-tailed bucks eagerly mark overhead limbs — even those that have been deliberately placed in strategic locations by humans.

THIS OLFACTORY

EXCHANGE

MIGHT NOT ONLY

FACILITATE THE

TIMELY BREEDING

OF DOES, IT MIGHT

ALSO FACILITATE THE

MEETING OF SPECIFIC

PARTNERS.

Impregnating one's own body with scent is chancy for small animals, and in diminutive deer we see scent-marking displaced on ground and vegetation away from the displayer's body. In large-bodied deer, such as moose and elk, which might have to travel long distances to secure mates, all of the scent is transferred to the male's body. That's why bull elk or moose perfume themselves with their own urine. The bull moose does it by pawing a small pit into which he urinates and splashes the urine-soaked mud over his long-haired bell. He then rolls his shoulder and side in the smelly mud. Cow moose really get excited over a bull's urine! The white-tailed buck does something in between dwarf deer and moose. It

marks its body with urine on the tarsal brushes and hind legs, and then sets up a network of scrapes where he impregnates the soil and his tarsal brushes with urine. A deer's tarsal brushes, a moose's bell and the elk's long neck hair fulfill the same basic function: They dispense urine-based scent.

Above: Lip-curling bucks might make a showy display. Once the female has voided urine and the buck is testing it, she is usually left alone until another buck shows up and courts for a urine sample. The female dishes out small urine samples so as to be left alone.

S ome fine work has been done in the past decade on signposting to detail and elucidate scent-marking in whitetails. White-tailed bucks approaching rut begin secreting from skin glands imbedded on the forehead. This scent is transferred to branches and small trees when the buck rubs, gouges and thrashes them with his

antlers. The more dominant a buck, the more he horns shrubs and trees, distributing his signature over several square miles. At low population densities, bucks travel and mark a wider area. Old bucks become active much sooner than yearlings and juvenile bucks. Shrubs and trees are not chosen randomly for horning. Small trees with smooth stems are preferred, as are certain species of trees, namely those with aromatic sap. Exotic, novel stems receive attention, but the buck is not overly choosy. Moreover, the buck might not stop with one stem, but horn several attractive small trees in succession. He makes his presence known!

In mule deer, the sound of horning is important because traveling bucks are attracted to it and use it to scout for opponents. That might be a factor with whitetails. Rubs accumulate where females are likely to pass, in or close to good feeding areas. Although horning and rubs extend a buck's presence over his rutting area, they do little to sexually excite females. That function is reserved for the buck's urine.

The mature white-tailed buck spreads his urine message in a highly distinctive, species-specific manner, which is called the *scrape*. The buck chooses a location under a hanging twig where he paws vigorously with his front hoofs, removing leaf-litter and duff down to mineral soil. Next, he performs the urine-rub, in which he impregnates his tarsal brushes and the exposed soil — an important point, as we shall see! Older bucks scrape more than younger ones, which is universal in marking behavior. Also, marking by old bucks dampens marking by young bucks. Scrape formation peaks about two weeks before breeding, a logical timing if it is directed at females, and females show interest in scrapes. The location of scrapes is specific to an overhanging small branch that is nibbled, chewed, licked, horned and painted with preorbital-gland secretions. This overhanging branch and the scrape split attention: Males inspect the scent stick, females the urine-scented scrape. The scent-sticks are widely spread and are examined and marked year-round by bucks, but scrapes are placed only under some sticks, predominately by older bucks.

Unlike rubs, scrapes are not marked-over by other bucks, or only exceptionally so. Bucks do not re-scrape a rival's scrape and urinate over his urine. Apparently, it does not pay for a buck to distort his urine message by scent-mixing it with another buck's. Individuality of urine scent is evidently important in scrapes. Females are attracted to scrapes and might urinate into them. Female

Opposite: A Montana buck mounts a doe in open country. During the excitement of the rut, the breeding pair might leave cover. Large bucks — often secretive — now become visible in open landscapes.

Below: A buck follows a doe in a deep low-stretched courtship posture. The female ducks in submission. She is close to estrus.

Bottom: A yearling buck approaching the mating pair is unceremoniously chased off by the breeding buck.

choice is strongly implied here because the scent in a scrape match-es the scent on a buck's tarsal brushes, but a mixed urine scent does not! The scrape is a female's guide to a specific buck in the vicini-ty. A buck mixing his urine with that of another buck's gains noth-ing. He only gains breeding success if his tarsal-gland scent match-es that in his scrapes. A female scenting a mixed urine scrape might refuse to urinate beside it, or wander off to search for a nonexist-ing buck, short-changing the buck who urinated into a rival's scrape. Therefore, it doesn't pay for a buck to scrape and urine-rub over a rival's scrape. Instead, he will scrape and urine-rub beside it.

In short, circumstantial evidence suggests the scrape is addressed to females only. Bucks must clearly compete with one another for females using scrapes, but females determine a potential mating partner by scent characteristics in the male's urine. We expect the chemistry of the male's urine to change with status and condition, and therefore, the female can choose based on such differences. We already know the urine chemistry of bucks changes with status. However, there are probably other chemical clues in the urine that reveal which bucks are the best fathers.

Because females get excited about scrapes and urinate in or around them, this olfactory exchange might not only facilitate the timely breeding of does, but also the meeting of specific partners. Consider a female making positive contact with a buck in the pre-rut, which she recognizes by his tarsal scent. Females avoid some bucks and run away from them as soon as they show up. Meanwhile, other bucks attract them. By running across a scrape-line with the attractive buck's scent, she just might urinate by one of his scrapes, leading to a meeting. It would be in each buck's interest to urinate in his scrape only. This suggests that bucks make positive contact with as many females as possible in the pre-rut, then cast their "scrape net" in hopes that the bragging and cautious courtship pays off!

Because whitetail populations in some regions show sharp genetic demarcations with habitat, the finding of habitat-compatible partners might be important in maximizing fitness. It might be that a buck's feeding habits are habitat-specific and are reflected in the chemistry of his urine. By urinating near a scrape, a female with similar feeding habits and urine chemistry facilitates mating with a habitat-compatible partner. Scraping might thus facilitate the formation and maintenance of genetic races and divisions, so characteristic of the white-tailed deer species.

D ominance displays are largely a male thing, rarely practiced by females. Scent-marking by does is limited to urinating in

Opposite: A large buck guards an estrous doe, assuming the accentuated erect stance and looking past the female. The female shows a slight courtesy crouch as she glances at the male.

Below: A large Northern buck at the height of the rut horns a hardwood tree. Note the massive neck, which helps to force deep gouges into the wood. His belly is withdrawn because bucks feed little during the rut.

or beside scrapes, presumably to attract a buck. Because does avoid bucks for all but a few days each year, their hormonal orchestra must temporarily undergo dramatic changes so powerful that they not merely tolerate a buck physically, but actively solicit him — all in the interest of timely fertilization. Conversely, the buck must suppress whatever tendencies a female has to flee, which she does when not in heat. In the courtship of a large buck, powerful elements of fawn behavior exist, as in the mule deer buck, though different elements. A white-tailed buck's advance is similar to a fawn's suckling approach, but exaggerated. He might flick his tail before an approach, much as fawns do, and he keeps low to the ground. His steps are hackneyed, emphasizing his crouched, low-stretched posture. Does he use the female's maternal emotions to approach closely? Bucks are eager, but do run out of steam. At this point the receptive female takes over with "coquette runs," as well as initiating strong body contact by rubbing herself on the buck, trying to mount him, threatening him — actions designed to arouse. It usually works. The buck displays, his advertising has paid off! After copulation, females might stand with an arched back, urinate and cramp their bellies. However, compared to mule deer does, it's quite subdued.

Dominance displays are a fundamental behavioral system in all vertebrates, including ourselves. There are huge differences in how such are executed, and we are a prime example. We fail to be grabbed by the whitetail's dominance displays in the first instance because we expect displays not on the broadside of the body, but on the front. That is, on face and head, chest, hips and genitals.

Secondly, we have not merely augmented our biological display organs, nay, we have made our dominance displays into an all-encompassing, sophisticated art form. We must have done this for

Opposite: A white deer — not an albino — at a roadside park, serving as a tourist attraction.

Below Right: A rare piebald whitetail in a captive Florida swamp population. Humans love to collect artful variations of plants and animals.

Below: White non-albino deer from a private collection. Such variants occur sporadically wherever deer are numerous. These deer speak of the whitetail's great genetic diversity, despite the severe bottleneck the whitetail population went through at the end of the 19th century.

so long a time already that our biological display organs have regressed compared to those colorful rear ends, genitals and faces of Old World primates. Never mind, we have done them one better by — at the most primitive level — enhancing the old biological display organs with showy dresses. That in itself is an art form we call fashion. However, we assert our status, our self-esteem, our superiority, with much more than fashion. We make into art virtually every aspect of our lives, decorating as we go. We take basic biological functions and make them into art. Eating and food equal cuisine; shelter equals architecture; sex equals romance, weddings and pornography; vocal mimicry equals language and music; visual mimicry equals dance, structural artistic rendition and workmanship; tracking equals reading, writing and literature; memory equals scholarship. And so it goes on. One can put it succinctly: The human species is condemned to art! And of course, we see art in trophy white-tailed heads, and we collect such and hang them on our walls for others to admire! What are those big heads supposed to imply?

Trophy Bucks

Why do we admire antlers? Why do we hang them up so we can look at them again and again? Why are trophy bucks the rage? Why the busy industry supporting trophy antler growth under private management? Moreover, it is not a recent fad — far from it. Trophy deer have been the subject of admiration in ages past, as far back as the days of cave painters who picked fine trophy antlers to decorate the stags they sketched on cave walls. They did not, however, collect antlers, as such were far too important as raw material for tools.

The late feudal period in central Europe made up for that. Nobility were so enamored with antlers that they built castles to house antler collections. They glorified trophy antlers in paintings and sculptures. They made trophy antlers gifts of state, and they spurred on foresters — who were the deer managers of the day — to produce more and larger antlers. And the foresters succeeded. Never have European deer carried larger antlers than those pampered stags from the 15th and 16th centuries. The foresters carried out their commands with a ruthlessness toward peasants that defies description. They probably had to, because failure to generate big deer and sympathy with struggling peasants could get them to the gallows.

Growing trophy antlers was a serious business that has survived to the present. Our infatuation with antlers expresses itself in trophy shows, trophy antler commerce and estates that raise trophy deer for market. Although medieval foresters considered their success at raising trophy deer a valuable trade secret, some pieces of what they were doing have survived. In addition, a number of successful attempts have generated exceptional trophy antlers. Consequently, providing one knows where to look, there is plenty of information about how to grow deer with superlative antlers, which is applicable to white-tailed deer.

What is a trophy buck, and why is it so rare in nature? Males with exceptional antlers — regardless of deer species — would hardly be a rage if they were common. They are not. Trophy

bucks are rare indeed in unadulterated populations. Yet, we now know it's no big trick to breed bucks with larger antlers in captivity. So there is the genetic potential to grow bigger antlers than normally found. However, it does not often manifest itself, a hint that trophy-sized antlers might not be all that advantageous to their bearers.

If we go into the fossil record of a species, we note there are periods when antler growth is superior. However, it is associated, without exception, with large-bodied males. That is no surprise because antlers grow with positive allometry to body size — the larger the body, the larger still the antlers. That indicates one cannot expect huge antlers unless the deer's body size is also large. This limits the frequency of encounters with trophy-class males, because deer are large only in parts of their distribution. However, even where deer are large, huge antlers are scarce. Nor is it merely a matter of letting bucks grow old. Bucks reach a peak in antler development that varies with species and population, and then antler size declines. We can safely conclude that even under conditions favoring large body size and low buck mortality, males with exceptional antlers will not be frequent. There will be bucks with fine antlers that are a joy to behold, but they will not be of record proportions.

If you compare whitetails regionally, you will notice differences in antler size. As mentioned earlier, whitetails from the plains and savannas tend to have somewhat larger and more complex antlers as well as more showy tails. This is an important observation which hints that antler size and openness of terrain might be related. And indeed they are, with plains-adapted species such as elk, caribou and the extinct Irish elk carrying the absolutely largest antlers among deer. Even mule deer, which inhabit the plains, foothills, mountains and other open spaces, has significantly larger antlers than white-tailed deer.

What functions do antlers fulfill for whitetails? As we already discussed in previous chapters, life in the selfish herd favors the evolution of complex antlers that can be used in head-to-head wrestling. In vigorous dominance fights, such antlers also serve as shields to catch the antler thrusts of opponents. Thus antlers function in offense as weapons, in defense to parry attacks, and as locking devices for wrestling — be it in combat or in friendly sparring matches. No disagreement so far. We then noted that antler size is a factor for bucks seeking seclusion in forest and brush. Most bucks carry antlers that barely exceed their ear spread. And indeed, running at full speed along a trail in dense forest precludes excessive antler width. In open country, wide antlers are feasible, but in dense brush they are a liability. Large antlers also cost a lot of ener-

WHAT IS A TROPHY BUCK, AND WHY ARE THEY SO RARE IN NATURE? MALES WITH EXCEPTIONAL ANTLERS WOULD HARDLY BE A RAGE IF THEY WERE COMMON.

Above: This collection of antlers is part of a massive arch on a Texas ranch. This old Western tradition has been captured by photographs for more than a century.

Opposite Top: Antlers are collected and displayed with considerable individuality and ingenuity — such as this antler tree on a Texas ranch.

Opposite Bottom: Even antlers of modest proportions attract attention and are displayed, like on this shed in Wisconsin.

gy and nutrients to grow. However, forage is not likely to be a limitation on antler evolution. Actually, despite our infatuation with white-tailed deer antlers, they are not large by deer standards. Following relative antler mass, the white-tailed deer is but modestly endowed. So why did mule deer surge ahead in antler evolution and not whitetails?

The answer is odd. The sheer success of the whitetail put a break on its antler evolution. It's only when whitetails venture beyond forests and brush that there is some selection for larger antlers. In forest and brush, they are amply endowed with antlers. Consequently something happens when deer move beyond their ancestral habitat of forest and shrub, and selection for larger antlers kicks in.

The most likely answer to why plains-adapted species have larger antlers hinges on the security of newborns — odd as it might sound. In open landscapes, fawns must be as highly developed as possible to quickly run beside their fleet-footed mothers to escape fast-running predators. This means the baby must be large to be a

WHAT IS IT THAT
MAKES US ADMIRE
ANTLERS? WHY DO
WE HANG THEM UP
TO LOOK AT THEM
AGAIN AND AGAIN?

successful follower. Therefore, one large singleton is preferable to two small twins. Also, the fawn needs to grow as rapidly as possible to survivable size. Therefore, the richer the milk, the more likely the baby will survive. Consequently, the female must spare a large amount of energy and nutrients from her body growth to successfully reproduce. So, we expect the female will look for a father that can spare a lot of energy and nutrients from his own body's growth. Antler size in males varies directly with their success at finding food above and beyond bodily needs. Consequently, in open landscapes, females select males with larger antlers. This explanation predicts that the deer species with the biggest antlers should be a runner, and it should have the most highly developed young at birth, as well as the richest milk. The caribou, the deer with the largest relative antler mass, exemplifies just that.

The white-tailed deer, by contrast, depends on hiding its fawns. The fawns search out their own hiding places, are virtually scentless, are called after long intervals to suckle, and then return to hiding. This must be an effective method to protect newborns because it is the most widely practiced form of neonatal protection in deer and bovids. It does not require big young, but quite the contrary. Small young will do. As long as the young are in hiding — no matter what their size — they are basically safe. It's when the fawns begin to follow their dam that mortality increases. With little or no selection for increased birth size, multiple births can be selected for. That's ideal for a specialized disperser such as the whitetail, which frequently exploits pockets of rich food. As long as does giving birth to twins out-compete does that give birth to singles, there will be no selection for increased antler size in bucks. A lot of re-engineering would be required to change whitetail behavior from "hiding young" to "follower type young."

Because antler size and complexity increases in whitetails from open savannah, females must have some sexual selection for antler size. However, there is currently no study demonstrating female choice for mates in white-tailed deer. The courtship of white-tailed bucks does not show strong components of antler bragging, unlike with fallow deer or caribou. It is more likely that female choice is exercised not for large antlers, but for males that are able to keep up with does in running. That would be a sensible way to ensure quick running offspring. After all, the essence of the whitetail's security strategy is speedy running.

So, how are some bucks able to grow trophy antlers and others are not? Note: It was postulated above that antler growth depends on surplus energy and nutrients. Clearly, bucks need a readily available source of food rich in protein, phosphate, calcium and highly digestible energy. We noted that such richness is restricted pretty much to shrub leaves and parts of forbs, and is not available from grasses. We can also rest assured that deer food capable of supporting luxurious antler growth is rare in virtually all habitats occupied by white-tailed deer. A buck can bridge some of the ups and downs in availability of high-quality food by depositing nutrient and energy stores in his body. There is also a demand side. The buck requires energy and nutrients for its daily costs of living, restoration after winter, growing a new hair coat, and increasing its body size. Daily costs might involve, among others, expensive running when escaping predators, the cost for excitement caused by human harassment, as well as the high cost of healing wounds and fighting pathogens and parasites. Then, there are the costs of companionship and of rutting. Predators and harassment might impose an indirect cost, namely, the buck avoids the best food sources and makes do with poor food because it cannot feed in peace. It can get complicated drawing up a balance

Opposite: In some bucks, the velvet at shedding is still well perfused with blood.

sheet of income vs. expenditures!

Growing maximum antlers requires a maximum intake of nutrients and energy, and a minimum in living costs. Bucks with trophy antlers somehow succeed in doing that whereas most bucks do not. Although this is correct in principle, it's the details that are the eye-openers. Because for centuries Europeans have had a keen interest in generating trophy antlers and have done sound research as well as management experiments on that subject, it pays to turn to them to understand what trophy management entails. The best information on how to generate huge deer trophies has come from periods when absolute dictatorships ruled the land, be it medieval nobility or Nazi and communist regimes in the past century. This is more than a mere hint that successful management for trophy deer requires extreme control.

The most successful trophy mangers ever were central European foresters in the hire of nobility in the 15th and 16th centuries. They were the most successful because they produced the largest antlered red deer ever, which is the European equivalent of our elk. Although highly secretive about their methodology, which was camouflaged in a distinct hunter's language, the writings of the time reveal what they were up to. Moreover, by the 18th century when feudal powers had been curbed, the first handbooks on hunting, wildlife and forest management were written, revealing an incredible depth of understanding.

The problem faced by medieval foresters was how to keep trophy

Right: Antlers grow rapidly, which is a unique physiological phenomenon. Antlers consist of protein and apatite crystals composed of calcium phosphate. A large amount of energy, protein and minerals are required for growth. The better the feed, the larger the antlers.

Below: The velvet splits longitudinally along beams and tines.

stags from leaving. Because of tremendous antler growth, the stags in velvet were exceedingly hungry and devoured masses of the best forage. If there was even a slight decline in the availability of high-quality forage, the stags would look for better pastures. And that would entail the wrath of His Lordship, and great suffering for the foresters who allowed it to happen. Not only did the foresters plant some crops and build wallowing sites for the stags, but they enforced, with singular brutality, access to the peasants' fields. Naturally, although such stags wiped out the harvest of suffering people, they could not be harassed under any circumstances. Driving stags off fields would be met with cruel retribution.

Not only must these deer have had access to the best possible food —natural and agricultural — but they could never be harassed, period! That's where the hated forestry laws came in. They were essentially animal-rights legislation that ensured game raised for the pleasure of nobility received the most favorable treatment possible, at the expense of the local population. It was treatment that led to bloody peasant revolts and deep hatred of wildlife. Moreover, in those days, forests were composed largely of mast-bearing beeches and oaks. These forests were rented out to pig herders, and the annual production of bacon and ham depended on this tree mast. The forests were open, and a lot of sun hit the ground, creating a productive understory. Game flourished in numbers hard to grasp today. When the potato replaced mast for pig fattening, the forest of mother trees was abandoned in favor of forests for wood production, a condition remaining today. Deer have changed externally to reflect the decline in habitat quality.

Above: Atypical antlers come in the most bizarre shapes and sizes. The cause of such deformity is not always discernible. Often, these odd shapes are caused by injuries to the antlers while they are growing.

For centuries, managers were aware that trophy production entailed more than continuous access to high-quality food. It also required removing all harassment, be it by predators or humans. While growing antlers, stags were not to be disturbed. In the first half of the 20th century, excellent studies and management practices refined the picture. Maximum trophies were grown by deer only after five generations were on high-quality food. The progressive increase in body size created stags rivaling medieval specimens in size. There is thus a "grandmother effect" involved. The key to large antlered males is that females on excellent food produce large, vigorous, healthy offspring. On the negative side, the deer so produced are sensitive to food shortages and quickly lose condition and health on even a small shift in food quality. These deer only live under luxury conditions. However, the most telling discoveries came by examining the demand-side of the equation.

It is widely known that bucks lose a lot of body mass during the rut, up to 25 percent in whitetails. Moreover, bucks are totally exhausted after the rut. Observations of experimental trophy stags

in Europe showed that antler punctures set back antler growth the following season — even though the stags had continued access to the highest quality food. Moreover, injuries attained in one year resulted in contralateral asymmetries of the antler the following year. That is, a severe injury on the right side of the body resulted in asymmetries in the left antler. It was then discovered that the wounding rate in the rut is quite high, amounting to 30 to 50 antler punctures. Little wonder that after the rut bucks look exhausted. They not only lose 20 percent to 25 percent of their body weight, but they also try to heal a large amount of injury inflicted with

Above: A Texas buck with a double-beamed antler.

dirty antlers. It suggests that the post-rut buck is not merely exhausted, but sick! It must not only heal, but recover some body condition before winter sets in. Maximum antler growth cannot be achieved if the buck is not in excellent body shape one month before antler growth. Bucks starting to grow antlers raid their body resources to get a good head start.

The foregoing makes it evident that for maximum antler mass, a buck must have access to excellent food year-round, peaceful existence to metabolize the food and grow, and abstain from the rut! Prevent stags from rutting when they are young, and they will use all their resources for body and antler growth. The result is enormous trophy males.

However, these large antlers come at a cost. Trophy management not only leaves these luxury deer sensitive to food shortages, it also makes trophy stags biologically incompetent. Their unwieldy antler mass dooms them to failure in fighting, and they are readily defeated by normal males. Should two trophy stags meet and fight, they stand a high risk of locking antlers and dying. Thus, experimental trophy males had a high mortality.

The foregoing predicts that the rare trophy male in a natural population is one who has skipped rutting and was therefore able to stick the savings accrued into body and antler growth. I was not able to study it in whitetails, but I did find this in the closely related mule deer. Bucks with exceptional antler growth were shirkers. They did not participate in the rut. They avoided conflicts with other deer, by avoiding other deer. They went about feeding, ruminating and resting in cover while normal bucks courted does and fought rivals. It might even be that by remaining hog-fat, the shirker can seek out more secure habitat than the active male. With a fat-load to draw on, the shirker needs less feed and can get by on poorer forage. Thus, the rare trophy buck can make a career out of hiding and might live on and on!

One can make such observations only on bucks that are totally tame, live in a large, unhunted population, and can be followed for several years. Mule deer tame readily; whitetails do not! Whereas conditioned mule deer bucks come at will to my presence, I succeeded only with one white-tailed buck in fall on the coast of Texas. He was a young buck and acted essentially like my mule deer bucks. I could sit a few feet away from him. However, that effort was for naught, because other whitetails fled the moment he and I showed up. Moreover, it is important to follow the same deer for several years, for in so doing the apparently obvious fell apart.

On the face of it, a large-bodied buck with huge antlers achieved such by opting out from the rut. That conclusion stands. It appears that trophy bucks are shirkers and cowards without biological

MAXIMUM ANTLER GROWTH IS NOT ACHIEVED IF THE BUCK IS NOT IN EXCELLENT BODY CONDITION ONE MONTH BEFORE ANTLER GROWTH.

Opposite: A buck's annual antler growth begins in late spring and coincides with the birth and growth of fawns. At this stage, bucks have shed their winter hair and grown a red summer coat. For early antler growth, bucks raid their body resources of mineral and protein to give the antlers a head-start. Consequently, the better the condition of a buck at the end of winter, the better its antler growth.

value. That conclusion probably stands much of the time but not always! A buck that I watched closely was a shirker for three years running, but then circumstances changed. He switched to become the most dominant buck that bred all accessible does for three years running. He was the most successful buck I have known!

Clearly, opting out from the rut, growing large and then dominating the field can be a successful alternative to annual rutting. However, it only works if the competition suddenly dies, as happened when a heavy winterkill reduced my study population. The normally hesitant buck found himself virtually without opposition and regained his spunk and confidence. I was a few feet from him when he lost his confidence as a 3-year-old. A big, regressing buck sent him head-over-heels into some broken aspen logs. The beaten youngster fled and became a shirker for three years!

It is ironic, but the successful bucks, the ones who have done the most breeding, emerge as old bucks with regressed, small, crooked antlers. There are important management lessons from this. First, one must not mange for trophy bucks. It merely produces handicapped individuals that are sensitive to food deficits and are likely to disperse, which goes for males and females. Trophy management invites genetic pollution by the simple-minded recourse of importing large-antlered bucks from somewhere else in the mistaken hope that it will improve the herd and produce larger antlers. It also punishes able bucks that have successfully exploited marginal habitats or difficult living conditions and, consequently, are of smaller body and antler sizes. The deer that will carry the species are the tough little ones that have mastered great adversity and poor living conditions. My hat is off to them!

All in all, white-tailed deer are locked into a biology in which males will have modest antlers relative to other deer species.

Right: When defeated, bucks turn to flee and are temporarily at a severe disadvantage. They might be gored by the winner. Also, a wounded buck might be attacked and killed by other bucks.

Opposite: Bucks that have engaged in strenuous rutting activity carry the signature of their breeding success in their antlers. Typically, they carry asymmetrical antlers of less than maximum proportions. These are the bucks that have passed on their genes.

CHAPTER 12

Closing the Circle

There is a great Circle of Being, which all living things are caught up in — us and the whitetail included. Look at the sunbeam breaking through the clouds, see the wisps of fog as water evaporates from the meadow to enter the atmosphere to be carried aloft by the breeze to become part of the clouds that become darker and darker till the water is sent back to earth as liquid, ice or snow. Here again, the water flows into living beings, becoming an essence of their bodies, of their functions and thus of their very existence. Red clouds at sunset are water that has traveled far, through many cycles, back to the very beginnings of Earth. And if water is not eternal, the stuff that makes it is and has been there in a mysterious universe forever. From that eternal stuff, our bodies are built as we eat and drink. What makes up you and me has been here forever and will be here forever. On Earth it cycles through life and death, through becoming and decaying, in a never-ending movement of matter through living beings large and small. What makes you and me real has been in plants and animals, in times current and times past, in fields of wheat and orange groves, in bears and bees and dinosaurs. We can follow the water cycle in detail if we care to, but there are other cycles of minerals, of oxygen and hydrogen, matter in various forms that enters life, transforms to support life and is then passed on to be picked up by other life.

Birth and death are mere process points in that Great Cycle in which we are all participants, be we conscious of it or not. We live because we recycle, and because you and I are animals, we recycle life through our bodies, and we can only live by taking, consuming and processing life. And from that is no escape — ever. Whether we eat a humble cabbage or potato, an apple, peanut or bread, whether we eat fish, eggs or venison, it is vibrant life that we must consume or die of starvation. From our body's perspective, there is no higher or lower thing to fuel and build us than life. And the truth of that conclusion is hardened day by day as molecular biology unfurls new insights that show just how closely we are genetically related to cabbages and plum trees, let alone chicken eggs and white-tailed deer.

The whitetail's ecological fate has been to be a predator on plants and prey to carnivores. Its biology is predicated on these facts, and it has been extraordinarily successful at handling both ends. In the whitetail's

cycle of life and death, its ending is the beginning for diverse, extraordinary creatures, one of which is ourselves. Whitetails have provided sustenance to North Americans for thousands of years. As people increased in numbers, so did whitetails. And it was no accident of nature. As the ice ages passed into a warm interglacial, as the old megafauna vanished, as agriculture blossomed and spread, so whitetails thrived. The archaeological record is tantalizing. It appears that early horticulturists, while eradicating large game that interfered with their gardens, deliberately cultured whitetails and made them a major meat source. Closely tended gardens and fields do not go well with buffalo and elk. However, they can be managed and made to succeed in the presence of whitetails because fencing out deer is easier than fencing out larger animals. Moreover, on the land beyond,

I LIVED ONCE FOR THE DAY WHEN I WOULD BE HUNTING DEER, AS DID MILLIONS UPON MILLIONS OF BOYS, AND AS DO MILLIONS OF BOYS TODAY.

whitetails can be encouraged by burning vegetation to foster the growth of abundant deer food. One can thus grow garden crops and crops of deer, and harvest both. Cultivating deer through clever burning regimes is much easier and less laborious than domesticating deer or other species. The archaeological record reveals how exclusive deer were as prey, and how much they were cherished. Even their hoof-bones were often crushed for boiling in stock. Whitetails were exquisite human food and they are still today. Then as now, however, they were more than food. Much more!

An American Indian friend, Larry Littlebird, once told me how, as a little boy, he saw hunters depart to go deer hunting, and how he dreamt of and longed for the day when he could also go on that sacred hunt. For sacred it was. It was shrouded in ceremony, in story and ritual, in expectations, and in recognition of the hunters. When they returned with the deer they sang, and joy and anticipation spread through the community. With what awe and reverence he touched the head of a deer, and how deeply impressed into his soul were the ceremonies that recognized and honored each deer taken. How much all appreciated the killing of deer as a continuation of their own lives. How welcome, memorable and thrilling were the first bites of deer meat distributed to the children. Knotted into all are the images of kind and wise grandparents, and the gentle, patient guidance they gave to him in making him a hunter. How much had to be learned! And how much they knew about deer and the land beyond, these warm, humorous grandparents, uncles and aunts, father and mother. They lived in deep reverence of life, taking nothing for granted as we are wont to do when shopping in a supermarket for our food, never shying from any task, no matter how menial, when it came to producing food. The very process was involved with the sacred, and with deep respect for the land and its living beings.

As my friend spoke, my mind drifted back to my grandmother as we went into the forest to pick mushrooms or berries, or cut tiny leaf-lettuce from the grainfields in fall, or pick little beech nuts that were later pressed for oil. Born long ago to luxury and riches, revolutions and wars had destroyed so much that was dear to her and had thrust us into hardship. However, that never bent her iron will or her optimism that there would

HUNTING IS A
SKILLFUL WAY TO
CLOSE THE CIRCLE.
IT IS A VIBRANT
WAY TO INTEGRATE
ONESELF, IF EVEN
FOR SO BRIEF A
TIME AS A FEW
DAYS, INTO THE
LIVING LANDSCAPE.

be better days. How much we loved those outings. How we thrilled to the beauties about us, but especially to the wonders of wildlife: the deer and partridges, the cranes flying overhead, the rabbit in the bush. I told her that when I grew up I would bring her deer and ducks! Heaven only knows where that came from. Wars, revolutions and dictatorships had stripped the family of men. However, I did keep my word. I, too, lived for the day when I would be hunting deer, as did millions of native boys in the Americas, and as do millions of boys today. And for thousands of years, these little boys were thinking of whitetails, as do so many today.

Hunting is a skillful way to close the circle. It is a vibrant way to integrate oneself if even for so brief a time as a few days into the living landscape. It confronts one vividly with the central reality of life: We can only live by taking life, by channeling it into the great cycle through our bodies. One can hide that reality by letting others do the killing and processing, or by denying the existence of sacred life by classifying it into higher and lower categories, sentient as opposed to nonsentient, to pray to sentient life and forget about nonsentient life. What hypocrisy! Life is not divisible. Only urban mindlessness can dull one to the fact that pulling a carrot from the garden rips a living being from its foundations. Bite into green salad, and your teeth shear living cells. Nor would it be worth biting into if the cells were dead! Hunting makes no excuses about converting life to food. In so doing, it makes us aware, whether we say so or not, of that greater cycle of processes to which we are bound inexorably. The deer's death reminds us of our own. However, it also makes aware that this beautiful creature, the deer I kill, will become a part of my body. I am part deer. Not an unhappy thought! I am, therefore, a part — a physical part — of that beautiful land I walked through, the red soil and gray rock, the crystal waters that gurgled from the spring, the tall aspen and firs that reached for the sky. Here lived the deer that has given me life, its life appreciated, thought about, talked about. Its venison treasured on the family table.

Hunting is a path of deep emotions, and I understand why people living close to the soil consider hunting sacred. I come from Europe, and from a hunting culture in which the sacred played a prominent part. Not only are there rituals prescribed for how to handle deer after they fall — rituals that honor life — but my thoughts drift back to small churches built in dark forests where mass was held for hunters, where their arms — boar-spears and deer-swords, ball and powder — were consecrated. I see in my mind's eyes the little prayer stations built along ancient paths in the forests where hunters knelt before dawn. Here prayers were offered to the patron saint, St. Hubert, the once wild hunter.

We all come from turbulent times that our ancestors survived by hunting, a continuous genetic chain that reaches back to the very origins of life. To be renowned as a hunter was a great honor then. Never mind other achievements. The successful hunter was a person of note and honor. That

Opposite: The receptive doe accepts a buck, which stands guard over her, protecting her from younger suitors.

THE DEER'S DEATH
REMINDS ONE OF
ONE'S OWN. IT ALSO
MAKES AWARE THAT
THIS BEAUTIFUL
CREATURE WILL
BECOME PART OF
MY BODY.

was the fate of men, to be judged such for hundreds upon thousands of years. And how hunting shaped us! How we came to be is as vibrant a scientific inquiry as ever, and hunting as a force that molds humans is one subject under constant investigation. It requires great skill to close the circle — even now!

I have spent much of my professional life watching animals, trying to understand them, taming them in the field to be close. I have seen among my students keen hunters who sold their weapons after a year afield living closely with and studying fellow creatures. I empathize with them. One of them whispered almost teary-eyed in deep, soul-searing agony, "They are so similar to us." He is right, they are. I do understand those who speak of sentient beings, who are overcome by sentiments of affection — as am I who chose to spend most of my life with and for them. However, I have not sold my weapons. I pick them up when the time comes, and I hunt and kill deer. I choose to eat meat, and I choose to raise or hunt it myself, and to process it, making it ready for the table. I have lived as a veg-

etarian, greatly enjoyed it, and moved on. And yes, I still enjoy the act of hunting. I enjoy greatly every lesson learned, and cherish each day afield. I know that the next time I hunt, I will return richer in insights and knowledge, and I am looking forward to that. I do throw in a handicap, as I like hunting whitetails the hard way, still-hunting, on the ground in thickets where they might sense me. There are more productive ways to hunt, I know, but for me there is no greater satisfaction than bagging a white-tailed deer in its own element. Yes, the whitetails I have bagged were memorable, highly memorable all. I have kept a few antlers, but three sets hang on the wall where I might glance at them during my daily routines. One was taken at 15 paces, one at less than 12, and one — my best buck —was

Above: Yearling bucks with short and highly asymmetrical antlers have a hard time after being separated from their mothers. Antler symmetry is an indication of health, and antler size an indication of luxury. Yearlings with large, symmetrical antlers indicate a good summer and fall with few upsets.

taken at seven paces after I missed him at 10! My last whitetail was also taken at those distances: a buck fawn gored earlier by a buck with three gangrenous antler punctures in its flank.

Remember Bambi? He is as cute and appealing as cute can be! The story is a fable, more in form than in content, which is weak and stands in marked contrast to real fables, which were intellectual tools to teach Oriental princesses the art of governing. Bambi's appeal is highly emotional and hooks into a deep instinct surrounding child images. How one trembles at the thought of sorrow or harm coming to something as "cute" as Bambi! And Bambi is beautiful! However, far more beautiful than Bambi is my child's recognition that a real Bambi is a fleeting entity, one that is bound to be transformed in its life cycle, that Bambi is but a part of the Cycle of Being, of growth and decay, of birth and death. Beautiful is my child's recognition that Bambi exploits emotions for gain, and that emotions arising, no matter how powerful, must never be confused with philosophy. Glorious is the recognition that

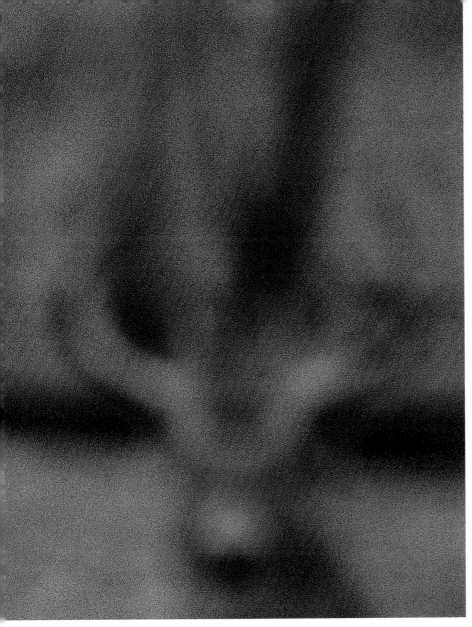

CLOSING THE CIRCLE
PROMOTES A
HOLISTIC VIEW OF
OUR RELATION WITH
NATURE, AND THAT
IS THE GREATEST
GIFT WHITETAILS
CAN BESTOW ON US.
MAY THEY THRIVE!

what counts is the great drama of life within which Bambi is a beautiful, but fleeting moment. What matters is not the mere ethical treatment of animals, but of life, and that ethical treatment is not in conflict with the taking of life. Ethics thus applies to particular circumstances, but not to the principle of taking life. Ethics applies to our dealing with the Great Cycle.

As long as hunting whitetails leads young hunters to such insights, it will generate sanity and stand as an antidote to the superficiality of urban based "animal rights" and environmental preservation — if one can call them such. Our current war on the environment can never be ended by abstaining from the biosphere's ecological processes, but only by reintegrating and maintaining the rich biodiversity that characterizes Earth. We must be an interacting part of nature, not platonic viewers of disjunct pieces of nature akin to art or cathedrals.

Closing the circle promotes a holistic view of our relationship with nature, and that is the greatest gift whitetails can bestow on us. May they thrive!

Epilogue

Why was the white-tailed deer so successful?

The white-tailed deer's success is based on its natural abilities and human support. Its natural abilities, initiated long ago, were honed to perfection by two overwhelming realities of North America's ice ages: a species-rich megafauna of giant herbivores and an unspeakable predator "hell-hole." Megaherbivores trash vegetation and landscapes and set trees and shrubs back to early, productive stages. They also churn soil through constant feeding, pawing, voiding and marking, which encourages plants to recolonize. If fostered, the whitetail thrives off these sites. No matter what ecological disaster, whitetails profit from it. They spread and multiply where species with fixed adaptations and movement habits perish. Whitetails were custom-made to profit from the ice age's unstable climate.

Because the whitetail was tested by many predators, it can survive adversity and quickly make up for mortality. When megafauna vanished at the end of the last ice age, deer flourished. When humans colonized the continent, whitetails profited from widespread burning and agricultural development. American Indians hunted large mammals, but must have fostered whitetails as an annual meat-crop. Whitetails became exceedingly common. This continued to the post-Colombian period when disease and warfare all but exterminated North American natives, triggering a spread of "wilderness" that lasted about 250 years. In this period, whitetails increased with European colonization. They declined with severe market hunting in the 19th century, but jumped back to abundance in the 20th century after the introduction of a continental wildlife conservation system. This system returned North American wildlife from the edge of extinction, creating abundant, diverse wildlife in the latter half of the 20th century. Whitetails took advantage of the protection offered by that system, and multiplied and spread as they exploited agriculture, forestry and urbanization. They spread northwest and are now close to Alaska. The whitetail's dispersal waves are exceptionally large, as are its populations exploiting rich agricultural lands. Whitetails became popular *Bambi* darlings, a reputation they risk losing whenever they exploit gardens and public spaces. This glorified deer quickly becomes a pest. The whitetail's diseases and parasites have also had some impact on potential competitors. Whitetails compete by becoming better colonizers, not by becoming better feeders in limited localities on unpalatable foods. This is a free spirit, without loyalty to any location. An exceptional opportunist.

Every year, the whitetail ushers in thousands of young hunters who are captivated by this beautiful deer but also appreciate the superiority of its venison. The whitetail, therefore, refreshes the ancient processes we have depended on for millions of years. Whitetails make a philosophical contribution of great value to modern life, while their beauty ensures we shall want whitetails for a long time to come. We might instinctively love species that are an ideal prey, which might be why we have fostered whitetails on this continent for millennia. We look after the appealing and useful!

Additional Reading

I have spent much time with habituated or tame animals, which is a great way to gain insights. However, it is only one way and it does not reveal how deer avoid predators. In part, this is because predators avoid deer in the company of humans. Following a predator on a hunt is problematic because a human can reveal a predator to the prey and thus interfere with the hunt. I have found it more informative to turn predator myself by hunting. That's why hunting literature is not irrelevant to understanding deer. Similarly, staying in one region reveals only part of a species' adaptations. Studying deer in different regions is informative, as is reading about deer through the eyes of different observers in different cultures and times. The more avenues of investigation, the better one's appreciation of whitetails.

John J. Ozoga, (1996) *Whitetail Spring*, (1997) *Whitetail Summer*, (1994) *Whitetail Autumn*, (1995) *Whitetail Winter*. Scientists who have spent a lifetime studying deer can be wonderfully informative, as Ozoga is in this seasonal series on whitetails. I highly recommend these informative, well-written and beautifully illustrated books. But notice how vastly different our approaches. Diversity is the spice of life!

Leonard Lee Rue III, (1978) *The Deer of North America*, **Outdoor Life, Crown Publishers.** Rue did a great service compiling information and presenting it in a highly readable form.

Sally Atwater, D. Gerlach and J. Schnell, *Deer*, (1994) (eds.) **Stackpole Books.** This multi-author book features many well-known deer biologists.

How I wish the late **Ernst Schaefer** had written more about his whitetail observations in the Llanos of Venezuela, and how I wish he had written in English! Schaefer was a keen hunter and a brilliant integrative thinker with deep experiences in Tibet, Africa, Europe and South America. A naturalist par excellence. He published his observations in German in the *Journal of the Berlin Zoo* (Bongo, 9:2-22, 1985). More is found in his popular books.

Anything by **Peter A. Brokx** is highly recommended because he did sterling work on whitetails in South America. Part of his work appeared in **Lowell K. Halls (editor)** *White-tailed Deer* **(1984)** produced by the Wildlife Management Institute under the technical direction of **Richard E. McCabe** and **Laurence R. Jahn**, renowned scholars in their own rights. See Richard and Thomas McCabe's historical chapter in Hall's book. It is a classic.

Karl V. Miller and R. Larry Marchinton (1995) (eds.) *Quality Whitetails*. **Stackpole Books.** For more technical writings in biology and deer management, I recommend the work of Marchinton and his students, including Marchinton's writings about quality deer management. Appropriately, the foreword was written by **Al Brothers** of Texas who gave impetus to this movement in North America with his own book co-authored with **M.E. Ray Jr.** (1975. *Producing Quality Whitetails*. **Caesar Kleberg Wildlife Inst. Kingsville, Texas).** This is a controversial subject, one with ample precedent in Europe, where it has a long history.

There are many renowned scientists whose publications might be of interest, including **Louis J. Verme** and **M.E. Nelson** on Northern whitetails, and **David H. Hirth** on Southern whitetails.

Dale R. McCullough, (1981) *The George Reserve Deer Herd*. **University Michigan Press.** McCullough dwells heavily on population ecology and demography — subjects I have paid scant attention to in this book.

Aaron N. Moen, *Wildlife Ecology*. **W.H. Freeman & Co. San Francisco.** Moen made a great contribution in this good, but very technical book.

Walter P. Taylor's (editor) (1956) *The Deer of North America*, **Wildlife Management Institute.** An older technical book of great merit. Great names of a generation past emerge: C.W. Severinghaus, E.L. Cheatum, Neil W. Hoseley. These pioneers created an understanding of whitetail biology and management.

David L. Mech and his colleagues contributed greatly to an understanding of the wolf's foremost prey, the whitetail, in many publications and a number of books. In Canada, so did **Cyrille Barrette** and **Francoise Messier** (Can. J. Zool. 60:1743-1753, 1982 and 63:785-789, 1983).

For a comparison and contrast of whitetail biology with its closest relatives, the mule and black-tailed deer, see Chapter 10 in my 1998 book *Deer of the World*, **Stackpole Books.**

John L. Schmidt and Douglas L. Gilbert's (eds.) (1978) *Big Game of North America*, **Stackpole Books. Steve Demarais and Paul R. Krausman. (2000)** *Ecology and Management of Large Mammals in North America*. **Prentice-Hall.** Excellent summary chapters on whitetails can be found in these books.

Many have contributed to our understanding of whitetails through the *Journal of Wildlife Management*, *Wildlife Monographs*, *The Wildlife Society*, *Journal of Mammalogy* and other journals, but also through state, federal and regional research reports like the following.

Paul R. Krausman and Ernest D. Ables. (1981) "Ecology of the Carmen Mountains White-tailed Deer." **Dept. of the Interior,** *Sci. Monogr*. **Series No. 15.**

Alan K. Woods, Richard J. Mackie and Kenneth L. Hamil. (1989) "Ecology of Sympatric Populations of Mule Deer and White-tailed Deer in a Prairie Environment." **Montana Wildlife Division.**

Richard Mackie, et al. (1998) "Ecology and Management of Mule Deer and White-tailed Deer in Montana." Montana Wildlife Division.

Otis S. Bersing. (1956). "A Century of Wisconsin Deer." Wisconsin Conservation Department.

Chester F. Banasiak. (1964) "Deer in Maine." Dept. of Inland Fisheries and Game.

Donald Dodds. (1963) "The White-tailed deer in Nova Scotia." Dept. of Lands and Forests.

Burton L. Dahlberg and Ralph C. Guettinger. (1956) "The White-tailed Deer in Wisconsin." Game Management Division.

Hibert R. Siegler (ed.) (1968) "The White-tailed Deer of New Hampshire." NH Fish & Game Dept.

Charles M. Loveless. (1959) "The Everglades Deer Herd." Florida Game and Fresh Water Fish Commission.

Most of the latter are dated, but are valuable in a historical sense. If the above appears a touch rich, brace yourself. It's a pittance compared to popular hunting literature on whitetails.

There are landmarks that stand tall, foremost of which are **Dr. Robert Wegner's** efforts. A former editor of *Deer & Deer Hunting* magazine, Wegner, a historian by academic standing, produced the ***Deer & Deer Hunting* trilogy** published by Stackpole Books in 1984, 1987 and 1990. These books introduce whitetails through the eyes of hunter-naturalists from centuries past to the present. I cannot praise these books enough. The excellent and useful ***Wegner's Bibliography on Deer and Deer Hunting*** was published in 1992 by St. Hubert's Press, of Deforest, Wis. Wegner was also instrumental in renewing interest in classics like **Theodore S. Van Dyke 's** *The Still Hunter*, which was first published in 1882. The foreword to the republication by Wegner, published by The Premier Press of Camden, S.C. in 1988, speaks legions about Wegner's grasp of the subject. Van Dyke, as Wegner and others recognized, was not only exceptionally qualified, but wrote exceptionally lucid prose. This is one of the truly great books written about whitetails and hunting.

Another old classic is **John D. Caton's 1877 *The Antelope and Deer of America* (republished by Arno Press, New York).** I highly recommend **Larry R. Koller's *Shots at Whitetails*,** and I greatly enjoyed **George Mattis' 1969 *Whitetail Fundamentals and Fine Points for the Hunter* (Outdoor Life Books).** Not only the past produced masters of deer hunting; so does the present, some of whom also write books, such as **Gene Wensel's 1988 *One Man's Whitetails*,** which he published himself (Hamilton, Mont.).

Larry Littlebird. (2001) *Hunting Sacred, Everything Listens.* Western Edge Press, Santa Fe, N.M. A wonderful little book for which I was privileged to write the foreword. Highly recommended. Here is a hand held out to us by a native who is a poet, actor, painter, author and storyteller without peer.

Popular interest in whitetails is being fueled by a large selection of outdoor sporting magazines. Foremost and in a place all its own is the award-winning ***Deer & Deer Hunting* magazine.** A succession of able, far-sighted and courageous editors has made this magazine thrive, among them Robert Wegner, Al Hofacker and currently Patrick Durkin. The magazine not only presents good stories about deer and the problems arising in deer hunting, but above all, it deals with topical and controversial subjects. It has attracted many good authors and the best wildlife photographers. The one person with the best current knowledge of white-tailed deer and their conservation? I would vote for Pat Durkin. Good articles are also found in general outdoor journals like ***Outdoor Life*, *Sports Afield* and *Field & Stream*.**

Anthologies also exist, such as **Al Hofacker's 1993 *Deer & Deer Hunting* (Krause Publications), Patrick Durkin's *The Deer Hunters* (Krause Publications) and *Outdoor Life's Deer Hunters Yearbook*.** There is no doubt that white-tailed deer have captured the imagination of North Americans.

About the Author

Valerius Geist is professor emeritus of environmental sciences in the faculty of environmental design at the University of Calgary. He obtained a Ph.D. in zoology in 1966 from the University of British Columbia after a six-year study of the behavior of free-living mountain sheep.

In 1967, he wrote his first book, *Mountain Sheep*, which earned The Wildlife Society's 1972 book-of-the-year award. He then took a position at the University of Calgary, where he became the founding director of a graduate program in environmental science. He worked as professor, program director and associate dean for the next quarter-century.

Geist's research focused on environmental health issues, which soon encompassed the ice age history and biology of humans. In 1978, this led to his most important publication, *Life Strategies, Human Evolution, Environmental Design. Toward a Biological Theory of Health*.

Wildlife conservation and management, in particular, wildlife conservation policy, also became an area of ongoing investigation. In 1999, Geist and Dale Toweill wrote *Return of Royalty*, a history of the recovery of mountain sheep. The book is distributed by the Boone and Crockett Club.

Geist has written and co-edited 15 books, and contributed more than 250 papers and articles. He also wrote more than 50 entries for 17 encyclopedias, and produced many short documentary films. His expertise has been used in the production of popular publications and films, including works by the National Geographic Society, the Canadian and British Broadcasting corporations and independent film producers. His latest technical book, *Deer of the World*, earned him his sixth book-of-the-year award.

Geist's wife, Renate, is a published translator, bacteriologist and teacher. They have three children and two grandchildren. He retired in 1995 and is now translating theoretical biology into practice. He loves to hunt, hike, fish, garden, brew and cook.

Acknowledgments

This book is essentially a detective story. It was decades in the making, and will, undoubtedly, continue to unfold. Many have contributed to it, wittingly and unwittingly: my students and colleagues, my wife and children, my friends and enemies. Thanks to them all! A question here; a comment there; a critique; a hunting trip or anecdote shared; discussions in classrooms, offices, lodges, checking stations and around campfires; opportunities provided, papers and reports sent — all sparked insights, provided missing pieces and led to "Eureka." I owe much to the literature, as discussed in the bibliography, and to those who took me along to hunt whitetails. And to those who critically examined my work, I owe a special vote of thanks.

About the Photographer

Michael H. Francis, born in Maine, has spent the past 30 years as a resident of Montana. He is a graduate of Montana State University. Before becoming a full-time photographer, he worked in Yellowstone National Park for 15 seasons.

Francis' photography has been internationally recognized for its beautiful and informative nature imagery. His work has been published by the National Geographic Society, The Audubon Society, The National Wildlife Federation, and *Deer & Deer Hunting*, *Field & Stream* and *Outdoor Life* magazines, among others.

His photographs appear in more than 20 books, including *Moose*, *Track of the Coyote*, *Mule Deer Country*, *Elk Country*, *Wild Sheep Country* and *Antelope Country*. This is the sixth book on which Francis and Geist have collaborated.

Francis lives in Billings, Mont., with his wife and two daughters.

Acknowledgments

Through the years, I have been most fortunate to have photographed most of North America's large game animals for book projects, but rarely have I traveled so extensively as for this project. I journeyed thousands of miles to many whitetail "hotspots" from the top of Maine to the tip of Florida, from the Upper Peninsula of Michigan to the Rio Grande Valley of Texas, through wheat fields, badlands, and the mountain foothills of the Rocky Mountain West. I wouldn't have had to travel so much if it wasn't for the fact that I wanted to show the many habitats of white-tailed deer throughout North America. I spent a little over three years on this photographic odyssey, but the photographs in this book represent more than 15 years living and photographing in deer country.

I couldn't have completed this project without the help, guidance, support and companionship of many fine people. As always, first on the list to thank is my family: my wife, Victoria, and growing daughters, Elizabeth and Emily. Needless to say, they spent a lot of time in Billings while I was off gallivanting in the field. I truly appreciate their support and understanding.

Thanks also to my mother and father, Derline and John Francis. You started me on this journey by allowing me to grow up respecting and loving the outdoors.

A special thanks to my "photographic friend" Mark Werner. I appreciate your willingness to share with me your "special places" while in the Midwest. Without the help and guidance, I would have had a much harder time photographing secret deer behavior. I'd also like to express my gratitude to the following folks for their invaluable help: Lee Greenly, James A. McAllen, Bill Silliker Jr., Steve Antus and Steven G. Maka. Thanks to all of you for your contributions to this book project. The deer have special friends in John Jorstad, Stan and Ester Stevenson, Dave Satre, Steve Hookstead, Ray Gehrig, Ron Pierce and the Gorniak family. Thanks for sharing your animal friends with me.

It is my pleasure to be able to share with you some of the 19,000-plus photos I've taken of these deer. Hopefully, between my photography and Dr. Geist's text, you'll get a feeling for the animal we call "whitetails" and for the places we call "deer country."